SELLING – THE MOST IMPORTANT JOB IN THE WORLD

Also by the same author:

Close Close Close
How to Win New Customers
How to Sell Your Higher Price
101 Ways to Boost Your Performance
How to Double Your Profits Within the Year
How to Get the Best Out of Today's Salespeople

SELLING – THE MOST IMPORTANT JOB IN THE WORLD

John Fenton

2000

First published in Great Britain in 1998 by Management Books 2000 Ltd
Cowcombe House,
Cowcombe Hill,
Chalford,
Gloucestershire GL6 8HP
(Tel. 01285-760722 Fax. 01285-760708)
e-mail: MB2000@compuserve.com

Printed and bound in Great Britain by Biddles, Guildford

British Library Cataloguing in Publication Data is available.
ISBN 1-85252-233-X

Contents

Contents

Why not use
John Fenton
as guest speaker or MC
for your next conference, seminar,
AGM or business dinner

'John Fenton is doing what he does best. He is selling. It's like having an audience with Billy Graham. There's a passionate promise of salvation in the air. His gospel, however, is for the here and now. Applied common sense. I am buying almost every word.'
Coventry Evening Telegraph

'We all agreed that, like good wine, captains of industry mature with time. You were terrific and already we are using your ideas.'
V.F. Giannandrea, Sales and Marketing Director,
Pocket Spring Bed Company

'John Fenton puts his message across in a way which uncomplicates the complicated and makes you want to DO SOMETHING about all the opportunities you let pass you by.'
Ashley Bartlett, Managing Director,
European Warranty Services

'Thank you for the splendid presentation.
All our customers were delighted.'
Raymond Mistovski, Managing Director, Facom Tools Ltd

VISION STATEMENT

The Profession of Selling

It is a glaring glimpse of the obvious to say that no amount of production is the slightest value unless the products are sold for cash.

Selling is the very crux of any commercial or industrial enterprise.

It therefore stands to reason that, as a nation which depends so heavily on selling our products abroad, it is very much in the national interest that the highest standards and the most advanced techniques in salesmanship should be encouraged.

HRH Prince Philip

Duke of Edinburgh KG, KT

Don't believe the Media –

Selling is the Most Important Job in the World

Foreword

What credibility has the Media – newspapers, radio, television – which crucifies Selling at every opportunity, yet still refers to it often as "The Second Oldest Profession"?

Note the word PROFESSION.

Okay, just like any other profession, including solicitors, accountants and bankers, there are and always will be those few bad eggs which the Media will be quick to headline. But notwithstanding this, let us not have any argument about it – Selling should be TOP of the league table of professions.

It IS top in America. Why it isn't in Great Britain and many other countries is more down to the Media than to all other reasons put together. And the Media has brainwashed the education established to the extent that our schools actively discourage pupils away from any serious thought of a career in Selling.

In the Vision Statement to this book, HRH Prince Philip, the Duke of Edinburgh says:

"Selling is the very crux of any commercial or industrial enterprise."

Positive, dynamic, enthusiastic Selling can do more to boost the economy and increase employment than anything else. And do it faster than anything else. In all walks of life, Selling is as essential as food and drink.

Customers don't beat a path to many doors these days. Only when someone develops something extraordinarily better or half the price of what went before. Everywhere else the inertia of human nature (bone idleness) causes the minimum to be purchased – unless sales promotion stimulates interest and salespeople convert that interest into orders.

In industry, if the salespeople at the "sharp end" didn't sell, just about everybody in manufacturing and distributing would be out of a job. Same for the service industries.

In retail stores and at trade exhibitions, if customers were just left to browse and salespeople didn't try to positively create a specific interest and help those browsers decide to buy, very little actual business would happen.

Author's Health Warning

Selling is not a safe, cushy job.

Selling is consistent, continuous HARD WORK.

But if the hard work you put into the job is EFFECTIVE hard work, not just the ordinary kind, then …

SELLING IS THE MOST EXCITING
THING YOU CAN DO
WITH YOUR CLOTHES ON*

*Listed in The Best of Business Quotations (Helen Exley 1993) and attributed to "John Fenton, Guru".

If you believe in yourself, you can achieve anything you want to achieve.

Chapter 1

How to Stand Out From the Crowd and Become a 'Positive'

You've got to be good.

If you know anything about Selling, you'll know that for the past 20 years the number of salespeople employed at the sharp end of commerce and industry, and in certain sectors of retailing, has been steadily reducing. Fortunately, due to the lack of younger people entering the profession, there are still plenty of excellent opportunities. Only in periods of chronic recession do these opportunities dwindle.

The reason for the steady reduction in salespeople employed is simply that salespeople are *expensive*.

For example, in the technological side of selling to industry, a salesperson will cost the employer upwards of £60,000 per year to keep on the road.

This £60K is total cost, not just salary and commission. It includes car, running costs, expenses, back-up, overheads, and so on.

At the same time, the average salesperson's time in this sector is spent far more on travelling and paperwork than on what the salesperson is actually employed to do: SELL. The time spent face-to-face with a customer is now averaging little more than 10 per cent of total working time.

Thus, for an employer of this kind of salesperson to achieve a satisfactory return on the £60K a year investment, the salesperson *must* be very good, very efficient, very effective, very professional at the job of Selling.

Just about the whole of the Direct Selling markets, where the salesperson visits the customer at the customer's home, suffer even more from this minimal face-to-face selling time problem because most of the selling has to be done in the evening or at the weekend.

To overcome the *expense* problem, most people in Direct Selling – financial services, replacement windows, conservatories, etc – are self-employed and paid by commission only. No company car, no expenses, no pension, no private health scheme – but no ceiling on earnings either. So if you are very good, very efficient, very effective and very professional, you can make a *very* great deal of money. In 1997, earnings of £150,000 a year were not unusual. Most very good salespeople who try commission only tend to stay that way, or go into business for themselves, which, if you think about it, is much the same.

In Retailing, supermarkets with merchandisers and check-out staff have mostly taken over from the previous 'Open All Hours' personal service selling in 'fmcg' markets (fmcg stands for fast-moving consumer good and, for some daft reason, is always spelt in lower case, never capitals). But in most other retail markets, such as clothing, shoes, consumer durables (stereos, TVs, washing machines, refrigerators, freezers, etc, etc) and service sector establishments like travel agents, hairdressers, and the like, the skills of the salesperson are still necessary – and forever will be.

In Retailing, the salesperson can get close to 100 per cent face-to-face selling time on a busy day. Retail salespeople are less expensive to run because they don't need company cars, expenses or as much back-up support. A good proportion of them are paid salary plus commission on sales, so they can earn very good money. Retail salespeople still need to be very good, very efficient, very effective and very professional – and if they are, they'll always be looking for the salary plus commission jobs. It is indicative of this money motivation that most of the very BAD salespeople you encounter in retail establishments are paid salary only.

Sam Walton, founder of the giant American WalMart Superstores group, said it best:

'THERE IS ONLY ONE BOSS – AND HE CAN FIRE EVERYBODY IN THE COMPANY FROM THE CHAIRMAN DOWN – JUST BY SPENDING HIS MONEY SOMEWHERE ELSE.'

The high cost of employing salespeople at the sharp end of the commerce and industry sectors has brought about the trend towards relying more on Tele-selling people and less on sharp-end salespeople.

Pure Tele-selling, getting orders over the phone, not just making appointments, is probably the toughest job in Selling. Employers are slowly realising this and putting their best people on this job, rather than juniors, with correspondingly higher pay.

Really good, consistently good Tele-sellers are in great demand and as rare as rocking-horse manure. If you can do this job and LIKE doing it, you're a star.

Problem Solving

There are – and forever will be – many, many thousands of selling situation where the field salesperson will always be needed to secure the orders. I call these selling situations **problem-solving situations**.

You cannot solve problems effectively over the telephone. You cannot even explain something technical to somebody over the telephone and achieve complete understanding. Face-to-face is the only way.

Most Direct Selling situations are problem-solving situations. Appointments are made on the telephone, but the selling has to be done face-to-face.

Coupled to this Problem Solving career path is the fact that, in Great Britain and in every other country in the world, there is a chronic shortage of problem solvers.

If you become one, the world is your oyster. You can literally write your own ticket. You won't have to apply for jobs; the best employers will come to you. But how to go about becoming one?

The First Step

'Do you want to earn twice the money you are earning now?'

The scene is the National Achievers' Congress, Singapore. Number of delegates, 11,300. The Indoor stadium is heaving. My biggest audience on the world circuit (so far!). My fellow speakers are Diana Golden, the one-legged Olympic skiing gold medallist, Norman Levine, the life insurance legend, Allan Pease, the world No. 1 for body language, and Brian Tracy, one of the greatest American sales gurus.

Brian Tracy starts his presentation with the question:

'Do you want to earn twice the money you are earning now?'

All 11,300 delegates roar 'YES'.

Tracey's second question: 'Would you rather do it the hard way or the easy way?'

All 11,300 delegates roar 'THE EASY WAY'.

'Okay,' Tracy tells us. 'All you have to do is find a few people who are already earning the kind of money YOU want to earn … and DO WHAT THEY DO.'

You can hear a pin drop as 11,300 delegates take in the import of this message. The inescapable logic. The sheer simplicity.

Too simple. Because for 90 per cent of the world's salespeople, the *last* thing they want to do is copy the more successful methods of other salespeople. This is against human nature. This is an insult to their **ego**.

It is much more stimulating, much more of a challenge, a much better ego-boost, to do it their *own* way, even if their own way doesn't work anything like as well as someone else's way.

Let me tell it to you straight.

If you want to be a success in the profession of Selling, you have to be in the 10 per cent, not the 90 per cent.

This is not a rehearsal. In Selling, you never get a second chance to make a first impression. There are no prizes for coming second – only for *winning*. You haven't the time to experiment. You don't need to re-invent the wheel. You use someone else's wheel.

That's why those 11,300 delegates attended the National Achievers' Congress. That's why *you* are reading this book.

There's more.

Never, never let your ego take over. Ego stands for Eyes Glaze Over.

If your customer's eyes glaze over, you've lost the order.

If your boss's eyes glaze over, you've lost that promotion.

Here's an interesting quotation for you to think about:

*'We judge ourselves by what we feel capable of doing.
Others judge us by what we have already done.'*

What to Look for in the Best Salespeople

If, as you read these words, you do not know of any salespeople who are already earning the kind of money *you* want to earn, here is a four-point shortlist of the most important things to look for – things that are easy to see. Most *really* successful salespeople have all four of these things going for them.

1. They are the salespeople whom the customers *like best*. (Ask the customers, they'll tell you who.)

2. They are always smiling. They spread happiness, not gloom and despondency.

3. They are always busy. Full of energy. They bustle. There is always a sense of urgency about them.

4. They are smart. They dress for success. This will also be reflected in the condition of the cars they drive.

Wanting Success Enough

So far, we've divided the world of salespeople into:

- 90 per cent who are going to do it their way, whatever I or anyone else may tell them.

- 10 per cent who are going to beg, borrow or steal anyone's ideas or methods or ways of doing the job *better* than the ways they are working at present.

    (Don't worry about the ethical issues when you are stealing someone else's methods. It is the most sincere compliment you can pay that person – to copy them.)

Please don't get uptight with me – but for the benefit of everyone, I am going to assume that *you*, the reader, are at present one of the 90 per cent.

The four books in this Profession of Selling series aim to move you into the 10 per cent.

If you are already in the 10 per cent, these books, when you have become a manager of other salespeople, will show you how to move *them* from 90 per cent-ers to 10 per cent-ers. These figures are confusing the issue a bit, aren't they? Okay, let's change the nomenclature. It is a proven fact that some 90 per cent of the people in Great Britain are Negative in their outlook and only 10 per cent are Positive in their outlook.

So let's call our Losers – **Negatives.**

And let's call our Winners – **Positives.**

It is vitally important that you can identify for yourself where you are *now* between being a total Positive and a total Negative. So here are a few examples of how Negatives think:

Example One:

Negatives will consider a trade directory to be so enthralling that every time they put it down, they can't pick it up again (sic).

They complain that, like all directories, they are out of date before they are published.

Positives know that every directory is probably 10 per cent out of date before they are published, but they concentrate on working with the 90 per cent that is still valid data and switch to another, more recent directory, every time one is published. They also carry highlighter pens and red marker pens so they can make corrections or add new information as they uncover it.

Example Two:

Listen carefully.
I want to sell you something.
It's something that will earn you more money.
It's something that will get you promotion.
It's something that will bring you more job satisfaction and more happiness out of life.
It's something that will get your boss off your back.
It might even stop your spouse nagging you.
ARE YOU INTERESTED?

Can you imagine anyone saying 'no' to that? In fact, our negatives would hesitate and say *'Yes, but!'* or *'Not really'*.

The world is full of them – 90 per cent full, as we've already established. Selling is full of them. People who work very hard at finding reasons why something wouldn't work for them in a million years. People who are so resistant to any form of change that they are in ruts much too deep to climb out of. People who have lost faith in their own ability to do better. Abominable *No*-men! (And, yes, far more men than women.)

Read these seven lines beginning 'I want to sell you something' again. Think about how they could be made to fit *your* products or services. Then ask yourself – is Selling really that difficult? No, it isn't. In fact Selling is simply applied common sense. But, of course, that's the least practised thing in the world.

Well, there's a smack in the teeth at the very beginning of this book. If you bought or borrowed it thinking you were going to find some sophisticated sales techniques to help you marmalize your competitors in three weeks flat, you're living in a dream world. Everything in this book is simply applied common sense: proven ideas that have worked for those Positives, the 10 per cent who seem to be doing so well.

Now I want you to be completely honest with yourself. When you read the opening words of this first chapter, down to the first question – ARE YOU INTERESTED? – what was your initial reaction?

Was it – 'Holy Moses! Just what I've been looking for for 10 years?'

Or was it – 'Oh oh! Another one of those books. Another smart-ass who reckons he can change my world'?

Or did you just read it with little or no personal response at all, kind of feeling that the words didn't apply to *you*? Which of these three reactions is nearest to yours?

If you got near 'Holy Moses' – great! If you moved the other way, let me let you into a secret.

You're Much Better Than You Think You Are

Or, to be more accurate, you're much better than your mind lets you believe you are.

All through your life, your mind has been building up what we'll call your **attitude screen –** that mess of experiences you've gone through, through which your mind lets you look at life.

You're already conditioned to expect 'No', rather than 'Yes'.
Want me to prove it to you?

Who make the best closers? Children aged four to seven. They *never* accept 'No'. They're old enough to use our language, but not old enough to have become conditioned. From seven onwards, conditioning begins to limit their potential.

Remember that day in the park with your five-year-old?

'Dad, I wanna ice-cream!'

'No, it's too near your lunch time.'

'But Dad, I wanna ice-cream!'

'I said No.'

'Dad, *please* I wanna ice-cream!'

'No!'

'I wanna ice-cream!!!'

'Oh, f'Christ's sake. All right. But don't tell your Mother!'

How come we can't be that persistent and positive when we become adults? Because by then we've accepted that 'No' rules, okay! By the time we're big enough to hit back, it's too late.

Throughout your business career, people have been telling you 'That'll never work in this business' or 'The boss'll never buy that idea', or 'We tried that five years ago and it was a disaster'. This is another kind of conditioning that keeps most people in line and prevents them from putting forward new ideas or from changing the status quo. Another part of your attitude screen.

Then there are the nasties. The embarrassments you've suffered. Indelibly engraved on your attitude screen. No way are you going to risk going through those again.

But all these things on your attitude screen are holding you back. You're much better than your mind lets you believe you are. Here's the proof. Read this sentence and count how many Fs there are in it.

THE FENTON FACTOR IS THE RE-
SULT OF YEARS OF SCIENTIF-
IC STUDY COMBINED WITH THE
EXPERIENCE OF MANY YEARS.

First time I was given this test, I got three. I read it through three times, not just once. When I was told I was wrong, I read it through again and I *still* got three.

There are, in fact, six Fs in that sentence.

The three you keep missing (unless you're a speed reader, in which case you may have got it right first time, because you scanned it, you didn't actually read it from start to finish) are the three in the words 'of'. This is perhaps because, when your read 'of', your mind doesn't register an F, it registers a V, which is how it sounds.

That's how much your mind is holding you back. An incredible 50 per cent accuracy! Maybe, therefore, when you start thinking of all the other ways your mind could be playing tricks on you; maybe you could be *twice* as good at doing what you do now.

Maybe for the first time ever, someone is starting to break down your attitude screen instead of building it up.

You've actually gone to the trouble of reading this far. Maybe you've even bought this book with your own money, rather than been given it by your company. If it's all making sense to you, if you're finding it stimulating, do you know what this means? You might be at risk. You might be a Positive, or have the makings of one. If you are, let me warn you – keep away from the Negatvies.

NEGATIVE PEOPLE ARE LOSERS!
POSITIVE PEOPLE ARE WINNERS!

Throughout this book I'm going to quote other people who are much wiser than I am. First quote coming up.

Our hero, a young man, heir to a vast family fortune and business, is talking to his beloved.

> 'In Africa, there is a beautiful and fierce animal called the Sable Antelope. They run together in herds of up to a hundred, but when one of them is hurt – wounded by a hunter or mauled by a lion – the lead bulls turn upon it and drive it from the herd.
>
> I remember my father telling me about that. He would say that if you want to be a winner then you must avoid the company of the losers – FOR THEIR DESPAIR IS CONTAGIOUS.'
>
> Wilbur Smith, *Eagle in the Sky*

It's a bit early for stuff like that, maybe, but I know it is true, having been through the fire. Most really successful people in business know that it is true, also.

I worry about Negatives a lot, because there are so many of them. I worry about where they are going. But more than that, I worry about how many of us Positives they are going to take with them. We are outnumbered 10 to 1.

Hey! I wanted to sell you something. I think you said you were interested.

It's a truly fantastic product. It'll really turn you on.

It's called success.

It's what I sell, every day.

But it's only for Positives.

Are you ready?

Positives Have the Edge. Here's Why.

If you are selling, managing the sales operation, marketing or steering the entire business ship, you don't need me to tell you that, with few exceptions, it's a **buyer's market.**

There are too many suppliers with too much capacity and not enough customers to go round.

It's likely to stay that way for a very long time – maybe forever! What does that mean? It means for most of us that whatever we're selling, wherever we're selling it, we're likely to be up against strong competition.

Times ain't wot they used to be. Times is 'ard!

But there is business out there. Oh yes! I know it. You know it. A lot harder to get it may be, but it's there all right.

This book is about *getting It!* It's written for people who *want* to get it. In any buyer's market, depression, period of recession, call it what you like, there is strong motivation throughout Selling for the Negatives to give up – to believe the gloom-mongers who keep saying 'There's no point in trying harder'.

The majority of Negatives in Selling have already, to some extent, given up. That's a fact, and it might include *you!*

For the purpose of this particular thesis, these people we shall call **sheep**.

Only the Positives in Selling are wise enough (maybe they've been through a few buyers' markets before) to know different. These Positives know what makes the salespeople and the buyers tick.

For the purpose of this thesis, these Positives we shall call **wolves**.

Wolves understand and use to their own advantage the psychology of the Negative, the sheep, in business. Sheep bleat a lot and do little else but follow those gloom-mongers. The psychology is very simple. It goes like this:

1.   RECESSION BREEDS DEPRESSION.

2.   DEPRESSION RESULTS IN FAILURE.

(Not all of the time – just *most* of the time!)

Wolves also know that when times are good, another series of actions and reactions take place.

1.   BOOM TIMES INCREASE OPPORTUNITIES.

2.   OPPORTUNITIES DEMAND POSITIVE ACTION.

3.   POSITIVE ACTION GENERATES EXCITEMENT.
4.   EXCITEMENT BREEDS ENTHUSIASM.
5.   ENTHUSIASM BRINGS SUCCESS.

Wolves assume that in a buyer's market the world doesn't beat a path to anyone's door, so opportunities are scarce. They know they have to generate their own opportunities. They know they have to find ways to counteract the depression factor.

Wolves set out to provide for themselves those essential four ingredients for success which you should be able to pick out from the 'good times' actions and reactions – ingredients that good times provide automatically:

OPPORTUNITIES
POSITIVE ACTION
EXCITEMENT
ENTHUSIASM

and they set out to do this because they want to win.

'When the going gets tough the tough get going!'
Lee Trevino, Richard Nixon and about 10,000 other guys!

The fact that you are reading this, I am going to assume, means that *you* want to win. Okay, throughout this book, and the other three books in this Profession of Selling series, I shall be showing you ways to make your own **opportunities**, ways to take effective and **positive action**, ways to generate **excitement** and ways to stimulate **enthusiasm** in your sales team and in yourself. I shall be showing you how to be a wolf, not a sheep. How to win the business battle. And I'm going to show you how *easy* it is!

Generating Excitement

Take generating excitement. As a consultant, I have been retained by many managing directors to help them revive their struggling and despondent businesses. The situation is nearly always the same – the people in the business are mostly Negatives, have given up, don't know which way to turn to improve things, are wondering how long the company can hang on, look miserable and sound miserable.

The first action I propose is nearly always the same. Warm things up. Get the molecules of the business moving faster. Generate some excitement. Get things buzzing again.

Then use the momentum generated by the excitement to do all the other things that have to be done. To try to do these things while everyone in the business is cold and stagnant and miserable is 100 times more difficult.

So my instructions to my managing director clients are these: 'For the next month, everywhere you go in your place of business – offices, works, wherever – you run. You trot. You bustle. And you do it at all times with your jacket off and your sleeves rolled up and with the corners of your mouth turned up – with a **smile** on your face. Nothing else; just run everywhere and *smile!*'

Most of them do it. Two days later, a couple of colleagues on the board are in the managing director's office asking: 'What the hell's going on, George: you gone daft or something?' George swears them to secrecy, and tells them about this idiot consultant. Next thing, all three of them are running everywhere and smiling all the time. A few days later, the entire business is vibrating. Everyone is wondering what's going on. They don't know what it is – but it's faster and it's happy, so it must be good news.

That's the momentum. Everything else happens from there – and everyone in the business believes that everything that happens subsequently has been well thought out before the day the managing director began his happy marathon.

We had a managing director once who point-blank refused to run everywhere, smiling. So we looked round for an alternative way to generate the necessary excitement. The company in question was in distribution. No factory, just a warehouse and a large sales office. Part of the way across the sales office was a partition wall that didn't seem to be serving any useful purpose. Joe asked the managing director, 'Would business suffer in any way if that wall wasn't there?' The managing director, puzzled, said 'No'. So Joe said 'Okay, Monday morning, we're going to knock it down!'

'Why?', said the managing director.

'No reason', replied Joe. 'Trust me, and see what happens.'

So Monday morning, the wall came down. And the vibrations started. Something was happening. The business woke up – and up it went.

That's how easy it is to generate excitement in a business.

And I bet you can come up with some better, or more original ideas than just knocking a wall down. Remember – *Nothing great was ever achieved without enthusiasm.*

If you don't really want to win – if you don't care one way or the other – then there is no hope for you at all in Selling. Please get out of the profession and leave a bit more room for those of us who do want to win. You're getting in the way! You're a Negative.

If you truly want to *win* – and if you work at winning during this 'buyer's market' era, then I promise you you'll become so strong that no competition will stand a hope of catching you up.

Do you accept winning as you main objective?

Do you accept the accolade *Wolf?*

Are you willing to banish all negative thoughts and actions?

'There are only two ways of getting on in this world:
by one's own industry, or by the weaknesses of others.'
Jean de la Bruyère 1645-96

YOU May Be Willing, But Is Your INNER Self?

There is one snag. Even when you really want to win, that insidious negative thinking can creep into your subconscious and screw it all up for you.

A sales manager I know who runs a large salesforce has a one-off exercise aimed at changing a particular kind of subconscious negative thinking back to conscious positive thinking. He calls it the 'I can't win with this guy' feeling. It comes to quite a lot of salespeople after they've tried for an appointment, say, three or four times and got a blunt 'No' each time. The occasion I heard of when he exercised (or should it be exorcised) his salesforce went like this.

He called all 50 of his salespeople together for half a day, telling them to bring all their customer and prospect records with them. They were all seated around a big hollow square table, the sales manager walking about most of the time. There was a bit of general business to get through, which took the first hour – then he gave his instructions:

'Sort out from your prospect record cards the six worst prospects you've got; people who so far have said 'No' at least three times when you've tried for an appointment; people who you know are good prospects, yet with whom you haven't got even to first base.'

When each of his 50 salespeople had done this, he gave his next instruction:

'Now, each of you pass the six cards you're holding to the person on your immediate right.'

This they each did. Then the sales manager pointed to the clock on the wall and shouted:

'Right, you have two hours to get out of here, every one of you, find a phone and get a firm appointment with those six prospects you're now holding in your hand. GO!'

All 50 salespeople sat dumbstruck. 'He can't be serious!' they were saying to themselves.

'GO!' the sales manager thundered 'Two hours – no more.'

Gradually, initially a few at a time, then a rush, which turned into a stampede, and the 50 salespeople were gone.

Three hours later, not two, they were all back in the room, once more seated around the square. Scores were totted up, and to everyone's amazement, the overall success rate was 160 appointments out of a possible 300. More than 60 per cent success – much better than normal performance in the field. And these were the worst possible known prospects.

On the analysis, three key reasons for this success were established:

1. The salespeople had no preconceived failure complexes in their subconscious. The prospects they telephoned were unknown to them;

2. They had maximum enthusiasm for the task, because they took it as a personal challenge from a sales manager they respected (that's leadership!);

3. Most of the successful 160 were telephone calls where the name of the salesperson who had passed on his six cards to the caller was used *by* the caller, as a third-party reference.

    'Your name has been given me by one of my

colleagues, Joe Randolph. He reckons we've a deal coming up that could save you a fair bit of money. Could you spare me ten minutes, say, on Wednesday, for me to come over and talk to you about it?'

The 'deal' they invented. The objective was to secure the appointment. They discovered that the name of one of their own salespeople was almost as effective as the name of one of their customers. They had plenty of time to think about what best to say and do when they arrived face-to-face.

So much for the subconscious negative trap. Few of this particular salesforce ever suffered from it again – and, from time to time, some of the salespeople even continued swapping 'difficult' prospect cards.

So to stand out from your particular crowd and become a Positive, don't believe what your conscious mind and your subconscious mind tell you. Keep an open mind…

These notices might help:

YES YOU CAN!

and:

WHY NOT, WHY NOT?
Sir Barnes Wallis

And a couple for all those negatives...

If you're not part of the Solution
You've got to be part of the Problem

and:

Whether you think you will succeed or not, you are right
Henry Ford

'He possessed all the attributes of a forged, razor-edged tool. The verve and confidence, the bright quick mind and adventurous spirit – but above all he possessed the aggressive attitude, the urge to compete, that is defined as the killer instinct.'

Wilbur Smith, *Eagle in the Sky*

Chapter 2

How to Develop the Killer Instinct

The term 'Killer instinct' might well put some people off. But it doesn't mean what you might think it means.

Definition

'The Killer Instinct' is a term sometimes accorded by salespeople to other salespeople because those other salespeople have an uncanny knack of winning orders against seemingly impossible odds.

And that is what we are about!

But unfortunately, the term 'killer instinct' is *more* often used out *of jealousy* for another's success, rather than out of *respect* for another's success, by salespeople who are themselves Negatives. Worse than this, it is a term used by negatives when talking about *the competition.* Just consider the demoralising effect this kind of talk can have. It's commercial suicide.

Negatives spend a hell of a lot of their time talking Positives *out* of doing anything positive. It's always been like that. Some150 years ago in the wilds of America, where the competition was *very* fierce, it was like that. Read this film script of the action as it was then, and think about it in the context of business today.

Film Script

(Sounds of galloping horses, whooping Indians, rifles and six-shooters being fired)

BIG JOHN	Well Old Timer, looks like they got us pinned down like skunks in a tar barrel.
	(whoop, gallop)
OLD TIMER	Yep, sure does Big John – I ain't niver seen 'em so wild before – do yer reckon they been at the firewater?
	(whoop)
BIG JOHN	No Old Timer, that ain't firewater fightin', they mean business and no mistakin'.
	(arrows-thud, thud)
OLD TIMER	Time was when a man could come out to these parts 'n settle. Maybe raise a few head, do some prospectin', make a decent livin' fer himself – even take a woman.

BIG JOHN | Things've changed Old Timer – these injuns are as cunning as coyotes and *(whoop, gallop, bang!)* meaner than starvin' grizzlies. They reckon they got more right to be out here than you 'n me.

(whoop, gallop, arrow-thud)

OLD TIMER | Look out John – behind you*! (whoop, gallop, bang)* Nice shooting Big John, but there's plenty more where he came from. I'm down to ma last three slugs – I guess they've done fer us this time.

BIG JOHN | The hell they have! I'll be a fly on a mule's *(bang)* before I'll sit'n wait to have ma hair cut by a bunch of savages! Let's see what they say when I git on ma horse and give 'em a taste of their own medicine.

OLD TIMER	Don't do it Big John, you ain't gotta chance against that number of injuns!
BIG JOHN	Leave me be Old Timer, I know yer mean kindly but there comes a time when a man's gotta do what ...
	(distant cavalry bugles)
OLD TIMER	John – do yer hear that! *(cavalry noise louder)* It's the cavalry – we're saved.
	(cavalry noise louder and louder to close).

If *you* were in that situation you just re-lived (did you see the film?) – what would you do?

Would you stay with the wagon train until your water and ammunition ran out? Would you hang on in the hope that the cavalry would rescue you?

No! Because in real life – in business life – the cavalry is just a figment of your imagination. You're kidding yourself. The *only* alternative to disaster is to get out and fight.

When you get determined to give the competition a taste of their own medicine, of sallying forth and tackling seemingly impossible odds – you've acquired the right kind of killer instinct.

If only these Negatives who keep getting in the way of progress would take the trouble to learn how easy it is to develop the killer instinct for themselves.

It's a mixture, you see, of just two things:

Confidence and determination.

The development of Confidence is critical and fundamental to success in Selling. And there are three kinds of confidence at the top of the priority list:

1. Self-confidence;

2. Confidence in the products or services you sell;

3. Confidence in the company that employs you.

Without the second and third kind, it is very, very difficult to generate much of the first and most important kind – **self-confidence** (unless, of course, you work for yourself).

Okay, I know what you're thinking. This is old hat. We've heard it all before. But what people do not seem to realise is that Confidence comes from just one place. Nowhere else.

Confidence Comes From Knowledge

Think back. Remember that feeling you got when you were face-to-face with that potential customer (we've all had the feeling at some time or another) – that you reckoned you were imposing on his valuable time? That, in his eyes, you were a bit of a pain?

Well, you got that feeling because of a lack of confidence.

And the feeling shouldn't have been there. Because whenever you are face-to-face with a customer or a potential customer...

YOU ARE AN EXPERT.

YOU ARE *NOT* THERE TO SELL YOUR PRODUCTS OR SERVICES.

You are there to show the customer how he can run his business more efficiently or more profitably; how he can improve on a process; how he can make more money from every metre of his shelf space; how he can *save* money; how he can solve a problem, improve his working environment, provide for his retirement, reduce his own workload – even increase his own prospect for promotion and minimize the risk of *him* being blamed if things don't work out as planned – by using your products or services.

41

You know more about your products or services than any customer will *ever* know – about how they can be put to use – about the benefits customers derive from them. At least, you *should* know all about it. If this isn't true, if you are not fully in command of this kind of information then, yes, you'll come over to the customer as a pain, and you'll get that 'imposing' feeling.

The customer will see you as the other kind of expert – spelt slightly different:

>X   an unknown quantity.
>
>SPURT   a drip under pressure.

Be the Right Stuff

Real Selling experts are just lucky – right? *Wrong!*

LUCK IS A PLACE – A PLACE WHERE PREPARATION
MEETS OPPORTUNITY

Anyone can do the preparation to make sure they are ready to jump at each opportunity.

Why is it, then, that so few people do? Search me! It is *so* important to get visits, particularly initial visits right, because –

YOU NEVER GET A SECOND CHANCE TO MAKE A FIRST
IMPRESSION

The first impression you make will be the one that sticks in the mind of the purchaser and will colour the way he regards not just you, but your company and your product, too, so don't underestimate how important it is to get things right first time. You never get a second chance to make a first impression, and the only way to make things go your way is to prepare for the meeting in advance.

You worked hard to get this meeting. Remember? You did the research, you made the calls, you put your case to a buyer whose first reaction was to say 'No', and you convinced him that you were worth listening to. You should be proud of all that. You are? Good. Now, don't go and screw up by going into that meeting unprepared.

You wouldn't be the first, mind you, or the last. Hardly anyone does the work they should before an initial meeting, and it's such a waste of everybody's time. But if you get this bit right, you'll be way ahead of the competition in a vitally important area – that of getting the order and keeping it.

First Things First

Research shows that your appearance and manner in the first few minutes of the meeting will play a major role in your success or failure. Pay extra attention to your clothes and hair, make sure you project the right image – a professional first impression, or PFI. The buyer must be able to feel he or she is going to like you and have confidence in what you say. No article can teach charm – you know best how to achieve that. Just make sure you're calm, collected and organized before you arrive and it will all fall into place much more easily.

Another factor in making the right impression is punctuality. Don't be late. But don't be too early either. You want your new contact to know what a busy and successful person you are, so don't turn up half an hour early and mooch around in reception, drinking coffee and getting on the receptionist's nerves.

If you've arranged a call plan for the week, you shouldn't have too much time to spare, just enough to get yourself sorted out, fed and watered, and ready for the next meeting. If you're going to do any mooching, do it in a cafe (watch out for egg on the shirt!) or in your car and spend the time reading through the information you have carefully amassed about your potential new customer. This is where you can take the easy way out.

The Easy Way

Go on. Take the easy way out. You'll find in business that almost nobody has time to do things right first time, yet strangely enough they do have time to do things over again. It doesn't make sense, does it? What they haven't realised is that it is actually far easier to get it right first time.

The same applies to sales meetings. It's actually easier to be well organized and to know what you're talking about than to try and busk it. Think of the time you'll save overall, not to mention the embarrassment and inconvenience, by preparing for your initial sales meeting. And once again, it's simply a matter of organization, and of staying on top of your paperwork.

How to Win Clients and Influence Buyers

Once you get face to face with that buyer, you have to be on top of your information. Particularly at an initial meeting, you have to gather as many facts as possible about your potential client and his needs. Okay, you're there to sell your product and yourself, come to that, but an important part of that is making the potential client feel that you are interested in finding the best solution that your company has to offer to his particular problem. That means listening to what he has to say and the way he says it, noticing what he doesn't say, asking constructive questions and making notes. This information will be vital to you in drawing up your selling proposal. The best way to store all this data and to make an unforgettable PFI into the bargain is to produce a customer file.

This can be as simple or as complex as you like – I favour a simple foolscap card folder. At the same time, it must allow the salesperson to present what he can offer in a clear and concise way. The main thing is to have it properly designed and printed, and to produce it in the meeting and start to fill it in once the initial

44

pleasantries are complete. You'll use it to move the conversation on to your products or services, to record useful information about your new contact, like when he takes his lunch and the best time of day to call, his extension number and that of his assistant or secretary and, if your meeting goes well, your agreed plan for future calls. Even more importantly, at least as far as your contact is concerned, is the opportunity it gives you to ask about the customer's objectives. It focuses the conversation on what's really important – what HE wants to do, to improve on, to achieve. It will certainly create the impression that you're really interested in finding and providing a solution to the customer's problems.

The next eight pages detail each of the four sides of the John Fenton Training Customer Care File. More about this in Chapter 4.

Five Magic Words

The customer file is a knock-out selling tool. Remember this when drawing it up – it's worth taking some time over. For example, you can include, as a prompt, a checklist of your customer's objectives with at least some of the five most powerful words in Selling:

INCREASE

IMPROVE

REDUCE

SAVE

GAIN

CUSTOMER

"YO[
TO M
The J

CALL RECORD

DATE	WHAT HAPPENED	OBJECTIVE FOR NEXT CALL

)U NEVER GET A SECOND CHANCE
MAKE A FIRST IMPRESSION"
: John Fenton Training Customer Care File ©1997

CODE

	DATE	FIRM APPOINT MADE ✓ TIME
,	. . . . . .	. . . .
	. . . . . .	. . . .
	. . . . . .	. . . .
	. . . . . .	. . . .
	. . . . . .	. . . .
	. . . . . .	. . . .
	. . . . . .	. . . .
	. . . . . .	. . . .
	. . . . . .	. . . .
	. . . . . .	. . . .
	. . . . . .	. . . .
	. . . . . .	. . . .
	. . . . . .	. . . .
	. . . . . .	. . . .
	. . . . . .	. . . .
	. . . . . .	. . . .
	. . . . . .	. . . .

WHAT THE CUSTOMERS SAY

"Since attending the Quoting Master Class on 7th October I have maintained a 100% success record in seeking and securing new contracts."
Martin Sewell, Chairman
Marketing Inititatives Limited

"I enclose the two forms which I started to use the day after attending your Master Class. On the first major client I have quoted since then, they were a resounding success. They became so fired up with our enthusiasm for helping them that we never actually got back to discussing the price at all!"
James Dubois FCA
James Dubois & Co, Chartered Accountants

"VERY good. Refreshed old ideas and gave a valued injection of Fentonisms. All parts were relevant."
Alan Pearson, Managing Director,
Thermon (UK) Ltd.

"MAGIC! Very helpful, idea packed, plenty of things every delegate could apply at the very next opportunity to increase business."
William Bryden-Smith
Technology Industries

"Mind blowing!"
Phil Cooper, Branch Manager
Abbotts Packaging Ltd.

"The most valuable input on motivation I have ever received. All of SIBMAP I found relevant to my business, professional and detailed. Now I can really get to work."
Richard Lamb, Managing Director
Ultra-Pro Ltd

CUSTOMER

ADDRESS

POST CODE   TELEPHONE No   FAX No

NATURE OF BUSINESS   E MAIL ADDRESS   WWW

PARENT/SUBSIDIARIES

SIZE (No OF STAFF)   TURNOVER   CREDIT LIMIT

TERMS OF PAYMENT   AGREED WITH   DATE AGREED

DECISION MAKING UNIT (DMU)

Size of company (Number of employees)	Average number of decision influencers	Average number of influencers who talk to Salespeople
less than 200	3.43	1.72
201 to 400	4.85	1.75
401 to 1,000	5.81	1.90
more than 1,001	6.50	1.65

Source: Financial Times "HOW BRITISH INDUSTRY BUYS"

STRUCTURE OF CUSTOMER'S DMU (NUMBER PERSONNEL AS BELOW)

DMU PERSONNEL	FULL NAME OR INITIALS	JOB TITLE	TEL EXT	BEST DAY AND TIME	LUNCH HABITS	AGREED CALL FREQUENCY	APPOINT OR PCARD	BIRTH DAY	OBJECTIVE PRIORITIES
1									
2									
3									

4	
5	
6	
7	
8	

CUSTOMER'S OBJECTIVES	*These are the objectives most of our customers want to achieve from using our training services, which of them are YOUR objectives?*	PRIORITY ORDER
INCREASE	Orders, Turnover, Profits, Call Rate, Appointments, Number of DMU contacts seen, Feel Good Factor, Market Share	
IMPROVE	Cash Flow, Presentation, Market Perception, First Impressions, Management Performance, Sales Performance, Staff Motivation, Effectiveness, Negotiating Skills, Closing Skills	
REDUCE	Selling Costs, Staff Turnover, Cost of Recruitment, Travelling Time, Mileage, Wasted Calls, Borrowings, Risk of choosing the wrong training, Calls to Quotes Ratios, Quotes to Order Ratios, Discounts	
SAVE	Time and Money	
GAIN	Up to 50% grant from the TEC, New Customers, Respect, Peace of Mind, CPE and Units of Competence for your MBA	
Any Other Objectives		

CRITERIA FOR ORDERING (CFO)

Here are the top twelve reasons why 7000 plus British based businesses decided on John Fenton Training.

How many of these twelve would be included in **YOUR** Criteria for Ordering, when you are looking for an outside training organisation to improve the performance of your people?

PRICE
Very few businesses buy training on the basis of lowest price. When they are looking for performance improvement, they look for the BEST value for their money.

TOP PRIORITY SUBJECTS
John Fenton Master Classes focus on a small number of top priority subjects and do the very best job that can be done. Highly practical training based upon other people's most successful ways of doing the job.

RESULTS FAST
Customers want to see results from their training investment NOW. Improved performance, more positive attitude, more sales, more profits. Every John Fenton Master Class focuses on the fastest possible results.

MINIMUM TIME OFF THE JOB
John Fenton Master Classes achieve in ONE DAY the same amount of performance improvement that most other training organisations take three days or more to achieve.

MONEY BACK GUARANTEE
Everything is backed up with a "no quibble" full refund guarantee if the customer is not fully satisfied.

	YOUR ASSESSMENT OF US (MAXIMUM 10)		COMPETITOR 1		COMPETITOR 2	
WEIGHT	RATING	W x R	R	W x R	R	W x R

MAXIMUM FEEL GOOD FACTOR
Your delegates attend MASTER CLASSES, not training courses, They are treated as VIPs. The venues are top notch. The Master Class MANUALS are 150 pages of really practical, useable QUALITY. Delegates work with unique hands on tools, like the STORY BOARD on Tele-Selling, the PPM System on Selling and the SIMBAP master plan. No other trainers have these.

LOCAL VENUES TOP FLIGHT TRAINERS
Customers can send their people to the nearest, most convenient venue, confident that the standard of training will be equal to Master Classes led by John Fenton himself.

SIT IN AND SEE FOR YOURSELF
Few training organisations offer this facility. JFT does.

PREVIEW DAYS
Every six months at most venues, you can preview all the forthcoming Master Classes in one day.

TAILOR MADE TRAINING
Customers can reserve a date and venue all to themselves and have the Master Class tailor-made to suit only their requirements.

GREAT ON-GOING CUSTOMER CARE
Your local JFT Principal Trainer will ring you regularly to check on the progress of every delegate you send to the Master Classes and to provide on-going help and advice on your future training needs.

IMPECCABLE TRACK RECORD
Every delegate assessment form is on file; every testimonial letter received from a customer - all open for inspection.

REFERRALS	Does the customer know of anyone else who could use our products/services?	Would the on our bel
NAME COMPANY ADDRESS POST CODE	JOB TITLE TELEPHONE	BUSINESS, PROBLEMS, SUPPL
NAME COMPANY ADDRESS POST CODE	JOB TITLE TELEPHONE	BUSINESS, PROBLEMS, SUPPL
NAME COMPANY ADDRESS POST CODE	JOB TITLE TELEPHONE	BUSINESS, PROBLEMS, SUPPL
NAME COMPANY ADDRESS POST CODE	JOB TITLE TELEPHONE	BUSINESS, PROBLEMS, SUPPL
NAME COMPANY ADDRESS POST CODE	JOB TITLE TELEPHONE	BUSINESS, PROBLEMS, SUPPL

For further information on ANY
John Fenton Training services,
contact your nearest UK Licencee

JOHN FENTON TRAINING NORTH
LIMITED
6 Church Row Chambers, Longton, Preston,
Lancs, PR4 5PN
Principal Trainer: ANDREW JONES
Tel: 01772 611115   Fax: 01772 611119

customer telephone the referral
half, as an introduction?

IERS, ETC

*"By the way, before I go, do you know anyone
else who might be interested in what we do?"*

"What do they do?"

"Who do they buy from now, do you know?"

IERS, ETC

"Any problems?"

"Who's your opposite number over there?"

"Do you know him/her well?"

IERS, ETC

*"Er, I wonder, I know it's a bit of a cheek, but you
know how difficult it is cold, as an unknown
quantity. Would you mind giving them a ring for
me, while I'm here, to oil the wheels, so to
speak?"*

IERS, ETC

"How are we doing, by the way?

*"Are we living up to what you expected from us as
a supplier?"*

IERS, ETC

*"Would you write to my managing director and
tell him?"*

JOHN FENTON TRAINING CENTRAL
LIMITED
8 Church Mews, Killamarsh, Sheffield,
South Yorks, S21 1JY
Principal Trainer: GLENN HARRISON
Tel: 0114 251 3116   Fax: 0114 251 3117

JOHN FENTON TRAINING SOUTH + WEST
LIMITED
9 Eleanor Drive, Bearwood, Bournemouth,
Dorset, BH11 9PB
Principal Trainer: BOB CATON
Tel: 01202 591778   Fax: 01202 591779

Obviously, you'll give this checklist plenty of thought to make sure that what you are asking is relevant to your products or services and to the type of businesses you supply. For example, the customer's objectives might be:

- To increase production/throughput/vehicle turn-around
- To improve safety
- To reduce handling time
- To save on maintenance costs
- To gain fuller equipment use

Make suggestions, be pro-active, but above all listen; the detail will be supplied by the customer and written in carefully by you. Once you've got a list of five or so objectives, ask your contact to prioritize them. This again will provide you with vital information for producing your selling proposal. But early on in the meeting you could introduce the idea of customer objectives like this:

You: 'I like to keep a file on all customers and new prospects. I find it helps me to give the best possible individual service, so I hope you won't mind if I note down a few things during our discussion.'

Mr Buyer: 'No, go ahead. But I must tell you, despite the fact that you said on the phone that you could save us money, we're quite satisfied with our present supplier.'

You: 'That's fine. It won't take me long to explain what we could do for you. Our products generally enable our customers to achieve five specific objectives that they feel are important. Most of them involve saving themselves a considerable amount of money. I've got them listed here. Can I ask you to take a look and say which would be relevant in your case? Which of the five would your company like to achieve?'

Mr Buyer: 'Well, let's have a look. Saving on maintenance costs? Can your equipment do that? I'd like to reduce handling time, too. Yes, this looks interesting, if you really can achieve all this. You'll have to prove it to me, though, with figures.'

You: 'No problem. All I need is for you to prioritise each of these categories and then to quantify what you'd like to achieve for each. Then I can draw up a proposal of what we could do for you.'

From here on in its up to you to make very careful notes of what the customer wants. Make sure you don't have to phone him again for any details – that would spoil the impression you've worked so hard to create: that here, finally, is a salesperson who is interested, well-informed and prepared to take the time to find out exactly what is needed.

File of Facts

Other parts of your customer file can be devoted to recording credit arrangements, terms of payment and so on, a call record showing the date of any calls and what took place, and a space for assessments, referrals and testimonials that you will hope, in time, to get from your new customer. Finally, you can include as a separate category another remarkable selling tool that will be discussed in the next article. This is quite simply a list of reasons why other people buy from you, known as the Criteria For Ordering, or CFO list. This is something you will be able to put together by talking to your regular customers when you visit them and will be one of the most persuasive tools at your disposal for convincing new customers to start buying your products, even for changing from their usual suppliers. It is based on a tried and tested formula that will make those vital first encounters overwhelmingly successful rather than the haphazard events they are for most people.

Basically, you need to make sure that everything you say and do, even the way you look, contributes to giving the – entirely correct – impression to your potential buyer that he or she is dealing with a real live SELLING EXPERT.

Ask the Expert

A real Selling expert show his superiority in everything he does and in the way he does everything. From research to closing, everything is planned and controlled to make sure that he is the Salesperson the customers can rely on to come up with the best solution to their requirements.

The *right* kind of Selling expert has well-developed research skills that enable him to find enough people to sell to.

The *right* kind of Selling expert has an intelligent and methodical approach to planning so that he is in the right place, at the right time, with the right information and, as often as possible, at the minimum of cost.

The *right* kind of Selling expert uses the knowledge he has collected about his customers to make sure that he is selling to the right person – the top banana – the person with the MONEY, the AUTHORITY and the NEED.

The *right* kind of Selling expert knows a lot – in at least five areas:

- **Everything** about the products or services; how they can be applied; how they can benefit the customers.

- **A lot** about the *competitors' products* or services – and how they compare with his own.

- **A lot** about the customers and how they run *their* businesses.

- **A lot** about business in general – especially trends in markets, and how *money* makes the wheels go round.

- **A lot** about relevant legal aspects – things like Health and Safety at Work, the Sale of Goods Act, Professional Indemnity, when ownership is transferred, etc, etc.

The *right* kind of Selling expert knows how to ask questions, how to stimulate interest and desire, how to talk benefits rather than features, how to match the customer's needs with the right solution, how to win appointments, how to close a sale, and many more.

The *right* kind of Selling expert has developed an understanding of Why people buy:

> The number one reason for buying is called in the Profession the DISTRESS PURCHASE – things like toilet rolls, bread, motor insurance, car tyres, batteries and exhaust systems. The customer has no option but to go out and buy them when they are necessary. The only decision the customer has to make is WHERE to buy them and how much to pay.
>
> People buy because of: fear of loss
>
> Hope of gain
>
> To keep up with the 'Joneses'
>
> People buy number one reason for buying is called in the Profession what products or services will DO FOR THEM, not what the products or services ARE.

The *right* kind of Selling expert reads a lot – and not just fiction – and is building on his knowledge every day. He knows how to use the knowledge – not as a know-all, a braggart, but as a confidant, who tries every way to help the customers – even if occasionally the help given doesn't result directly in business. There is no harm in sowing the seeds that can be reaped later – but always with an eye on future business.

THOSE WHO DON'T READ BOOKS HAVE NO ADVANTAGE
OVER THOSE WHO CAN'T.

Once you have cracked this knowledge factor and can honestly call yourself an expert – I promise you, you'll never get that feeling of imposing yourself on a customer – of wasting his time – ever again.

This will bring you most of the Confidence you need.

The *right* kind of Selling expert has realised that all these skills will add up to the greatest attribute of all:

TO BE THE SALESPERSON THE CUSTOMERS LIKE BEST

Because the most important factor of all in selling is that:

PEOPLE BUY PEOPLE FIRST

Investing in Training

It never ceases to amaze me how many companies send their salespeople out to sell to customers without any more than a superficial injection of knowledge.

One week! Two at the most of product training.

Nothing on the competitors. Nothing on the kind of customers they will be calling on. Nothing on business in general and what makes the wheels of industry go round.

Is it any wonder, therefore, that so many salespeople fail? It isn't their fault; it's the fault of the companies that employ them. There just isn't any substitute for knowledge.

At this point there are going to be umpteen sales directors throwing their hands in the air and shouting, 'That's all very well, but how do we find the time to do all this knowledge training, and where does the money come from to allow us to make it happen?'

Valid point. In the real world there is never enough time to do everything you need to do. But hold on, remember that old saying:

THERE'S NEVER TIME TO DO IT RIGHT, BUT THERE'S
ALWAYS TIME TO DO IT AGAIN!

We are talking here about *losing business* because of not doing it right. There may not be *an opportunity* to do it again. Where does *that* stand in your priority list?

There is one way to shorten the knowledge learning curve and inject the required amount of product, application, benefit, competition, customer and business knowledge into a salesforce *faster* and at much less cost. This is what I call it.

A Day's Worth of USP

USP stands for **Unique Selling Point.** It was all the rage before someone invented the word 'Marketing' and fudged everything.

USP is the difference, the edge you've got over your competitors. It's likely to be different for each product or service, against each competitor. If you don't know – in fine detail – what your USP is, then you can't sell successfully against competition.

Finding out what your USP is, if you are a sales manager, also gives your salesforce all that essential knowledge they need, from which they build their confidence.

Let's assume you *are* a sales manager. Call a meeting. Take a room for a day – big enough for your entire salesforce – new recruits, trainees and all the old hands. Cover the walls of the room with blank flip charts. You'll need at least 10, and 20 would be better.

You've told your salesforce to be there at 9.00am sharp for the meeting, but you haven't told them why. Introductions over, you start the ball rolling:

> 'Okay team, we're going to spend the entire morning answering in fine detail just one question. The answer we're going to write on these flip charts around the walls – and I expect to fill every single one.
>
> The question is:
>
> WHY DO PEOPLE BUY FROM US?'

The first 10 minutes will be easy. All the old chestnuts will come out. 'We're best.' 'We're oldest established.' 'The customers know us.' 'They know the product's a proven seller.' Lists begin to develop on the flip charts, but the answers at this early stage will be rather too superficial, too broad, lacking depth. So you begin to question each answer, using that very useful key word – **why?**

And gradually, the superficial answers will grow roots and the *real* reasons will be uncovered. Then you begin separating each product and each type of customer or application – and your team begins to see that a certain USP for one product does not apply to another. And certain types of customers appreciate certain aspects of certain products, while for other customers those aspects are irrelevant.

The pace of the meeting will quicken, as the members of your team get the hang of it and realize what's going on. The old hands contribute the most, of course, and the new recruits learn things they wouldn't learn in a month of Sundays out in the field. By lunchtime, every flip chart is filled.

The following statements were developed during a one-hour 'Why do people buy from us?' session led by John Fenton for Oddbins Ltd, Corporate Business Sales Team. They show just how comprehensive and detailed the results of this kind of brainstorming process can be.

- One *local* telephone call for EVERYTHING. And the local people *know* everything about you – as a Corporate customer.

- The product range is EXCITING, INNOVATIVE – VERY DIFFERENT from your bog-standard wine merchant.

- We are the market leaders, the trendsetters.

- We make our *customers* stand out and be different.

- We can design and produce your Wine Lists, blackboards, organize tastings, educate your staff. Any time you like, you can visit your local branch for a tasting.

- You share in our reputation and success for the most exciting 'Bin-ends' which you can regularly add to your on-going Wine list to tickle your customers' fancy.

- Big groups can run a National Account on a local basis.

- We talk your language.

- We are very nice people to do business with. We'll make you feel good, not make you feel miserable.
- We run an extensive gift voucher, Christmas boxes, and incentive scheme service for *your* customers or staff.
- *YOUR* needs are our concern. We do not put obstacles in the way – we make things happen.
- We love *joint* ventures.
- We can give you a better class of customer – the people who spend more. When your customers know you use *Oddbins*, other things will happen.
- Why? Because we are *Which* magazine's National High Street Wine Merchant of the Year – and have been for the last three years.
- We have been the International Wine Challenge 'Wine Merchant of the Year' for five consecutive years. We didn't win last year – because they didn't allow us to enter. 'Give someone else a chance', they said.
- Our annual Wine Fairs are major events in the international wine business. All our new Corporate customers are invited, *free*.
- You will never find such enthusiasm and dedication anywhere else.
- We care. We believe.
- All our Corporate Account Managers are wine experts – and there is *nothing* in our range that they wouldn't happily drink themselves.
- Our branch is like having your own cellar, but just around the corner. With your bog-standard wine merchant you might wait a week and can only contact them 9-5 Monday to Friday. With us, you can get your emergency supplies 10am-10pm Monday to Saturday AND 12-3pm on Sunday.
- We trust you! You get corporate prices from the word go.
- Our range is so wide that we can give two or three customers in the same area each a totally different but equally exciting Wine List.

- You can buy a single bottle or 100 cases – only factor is a £50 minimum order value.
- You get full Sale or Return facilities and glasses service for functions.

With the same approach, you could develop a similar list that will make your customers just as enthusiastic as you are about what your product can do for them.

After a good lunch (but not too good!) the team reconvenes. During the lunch break, all the used flip charts have been replaced with fresh blank ones. The used ones lie on the floor all round the room.

You lead off again:

'Right team, this afternoon we are again going to devote entirely to answering just one question, in the same kind of fine detail as this morning. The question this time is:
WHY DO PEOPLE BUY FROM OUR COMPETITORS?'

The team sets off at a much brisker pace. The usual chestnuts again come out first: 'Their prices are lower,' 'Their delivery is shorter.' 'They spend more on booze and entertainment than we do.' 'Their advertising is more effective.'

Again you question the superficial chestnuts. 'Do *all* our competitors have lower prices than ours?' Of course they don't. So you separate those that do from those that don't. 'Can all our competitors deliver quicker, or does this only apply to certain areas at certain times?'

'How important is the entertainment factor, compared with the tangible cost-saving benefits?' 'Which of our competitors truly beat us on advertising and which do *we* beat?'

Separate lists grow and grow. And as they do, one thing becomes all too clear – most of the answers in the afternoon look pretty much the same as the answers in the morning's session. So about teatime the morning's flip charts come up again off the floor to be matched against the afternoon's and any identical answers are cancelled out by striking a line through them.

By the end of the day, the *true* USP – your **true selling edge –** will have been established for at least your three main products or services, when sold to your three main types of customer, when up against your three main competitors. That will be 3 x 3 x 3 = 27 variations of USP – and you won't win all 27. For some you'll clearly see that your competition has the edge. But you'll also see clearly what you have to do to *improve* your USP and get back on the winning side.

Every member of your team, old hands as well as new recruits, will leave that room with more product, customer and competition knowledge than you'll ever inject through the usual style of product training sessions. And after that first day, you'll arrange other days, probably once a month, because most of you have a lot *more* than three main products, types of customers and competitors. If you have *six* of each, your possible variations of USP are 6 x 6 x 6 = 216. So that's your monthly sales meetings sorted out for at least the next year. But it won't take a whole day after the first meeting. They know what to expect and will prepare accordingly. Two hours should get you another 27 variations each month.

Now, all you individual Salespeople out there – don't wait for your sales manager to call the meeting. Get cracking yourself. The meeting might never happen otherwise, and that's a hell of a lousy reason to stay ignorant!

Let's recap.

We are looking at how to develop the killer instinct and we've now covered the first of the two key factors:

Confidence which comes from knowledge.

So let's look at the second key factor.

Determination

The easiest way to get to grips with the development of determination is never to forget what I see as the first law of Selling:

THERE ARE NO PRIZES FOR THE SELLER WHO COMES SECOND.

You won't last long in this business if you see yourself as a kind of benevolent consultant, keen to offer advice and help, but without an eye, an ear and a nose for *business*. Determination means that once you are in there – an expert who has found a need and is working hard at fulfilling it with *your* product of service – you don't give up when the customer says: 'I'm not really interested,' or 'It's too much trouble to change all that'.

Even if a customer gives you a direct 'NO'; with determination you don't take 'No' for an answer unless you are sure of his reasons for saying 'No' and, even then, only if they are v*alid* reasons. (Remember what you could do when you were five?)

Perhaps your knowledge of the situation, or even just your instinct, gives you the feeling that he's putting you off – that there is something behind his resistance that he's not coming clean about. You get determined to find out what that something is – after all, he's got no right to mess you about after you've spent all that time trying to help him. You've got a right to some kind of return, or at least the satisfaction of knowing the *real* reason why you failed – so that you can avoid making the same mistake again. But you do *not* get aggressive. You don't get annoyed with the customer.

You keep your cool and you *probe*. You ask the customer questions like:

'When you say you're not interested, does that mean you've found a better way of doing it than we can give you?'

If the customer says 'No', which he almost certainly will, you follow up with: 'Well, if you haven't found a better way, what do you mean?' And for the too-much-trouble situation: 'When you say it's too much trouble, do you mean the savings won't cover the costs of changing over?'

This will leave him speechless and rubbing his chin, so you follow up with:

'Well, okay then, let's establish the break-even point and see if we can improve things'.

Here's a dilly for when the hold up is just *him:* 'Is there anyone else in your company likely to put obstacles in the way of progress, for purely selfish reasons, if you go ahead? Are you saying no because of this?'

He'll think of everyone who might conceivably point the finger at him and his 'political' resistance will quite often disappear.

Or you can look the customer straight in the eye and say: 'We've established that there are real savings if you use this equipment, so how can you give me a straight **no?** I'd appreciate knowing your reasons for turning me down'.

That's **determination.** And when you have determination backed by Confidence and Knowledge, if you come upon a situation where you establish that you *cannot* be of help to a customer, he doesn't have to tell *you* that – you tell *him*.

There are no short cuts that I know of, other than the day's worth of USP. If you don't know what you are selling and why people will buy it, you won't develop the killer instinct, you'll develop the *suicide* instinct, and likely as not you'll finish up down the pan!

As well as believing in your product, you have to believe in yourself and in your innate ability to be the best. If you don't truly believe that you can do it, you'll find yourself failing to achieve your true potential, despite all the determination and preparation in the world. But you can work on it – let me show you how.

Chapter 3
Starting the Day Right

Some days everything goes right – you feel good, you know you look good, customers respond to you in just the way you want and orders drop into your lap, even traffic wardens smile at you. On days like that, you could ask for the moon and end up with some stars thrown in for free. Other days – well, let's just say that we've all experienced those heart-sink days, that just go on getting worse from the first outright rejection to the last missed appointment. It's happened to everyone at some time or other, and most people just put it down to good or bad luck, and leave it at that. But, incredible though it may seem, you can take charge of your performance and, by turning your aspirations into reality, make sure every day is your lucky day with results to match.

To perform at your peak as a salesperson, you have to start off the day right. Start off by doing everything you can to feel *positive* about yourself, your company, your product and your unique role in helping buyers to solve their problems.

Don't put obstacles in your way –

Don't … listen to the News when you wake up

Or read the newspapers

It's all BAD NEWS and you don't need it.

Take a hint from Christine Cartwright, top business development manager for Estee Lauder. Truly a star among stars – she certainly knows what she's talking about:

'When you wake up in the morning, what do you need?…
CONFIDENCE.
What's the first Selling job you have to do – at twenty past six or thereabouts?

It's on your right leg – to get it out of bed.

Next – you need a pee – to get rid of the waste.

Next – you need a cup of tea or coffee – to ACTIVATE.

After that, you need to put all the other bits of your CONFIDENCE together so that you can face the world – and your customers.

Do a lousy selling job on your right leg – steal that extra 20 minutes between the sheets – and when you DO stagger out of bed to the loo – you're LATE.

You're RUSHED.

You slosh through your ablutions, half clean your teeth, grab whatever clothes you can find, skip breakfast and finally get to your car.

How do you feel?

And how do you feel for the rest of the day?

HORRIBLE!

YOUR OTHER BITS OF CONFIDENCE...

By the time you got into the bathroom this morning, how many people in your house had told you that you were:

> Bubbleicious
>
> Delicious
>
> Gorgeous
>
> Unique and
>
> Valuable?

Okay, if nobody tells YOU – you look into the bathroom mirror and you tell YOURSELF.'

Your bathroom mirror is the most important object in your home. Every single morning of your life, you look at yourself in that mirror and contemplate the day ahead.

What you *should* be doing is *using* the bathroom mirror. Like Shirley Valentine used her kitchen wall. You should be talking to yourself as you *look* at yourself each morning. You should be telling youself – *yelling* at yourself several times, 'I FEEL TERRRRIIIIFFFIIIICCC!' and punching the air. (Do this and for the first week at least it'll keep your screaming kids out of the way till you've left for work!)

Ladies use their bathroom mirror to put on the face with which they face the world.

Fellers use their bathroom mirror to practise *smiling* and to talk themselves *up*.

Starting the Day Right in Tele-Selling

Do you like sport? If you play tennis, squash, football or anything similar, you know what those first few minutes on the court of the field are like if you haven't warmed up.

If you know any really good musicians, you'll know also that they practise for hours every day.

So what of the professional tele-selling person and the warm-up at the start of play?

If you begin selling – making your tele-calls – at the start of the day without any warm-up at all, then your first three or four calls of the day ARE your warm-up. Like it or not, those first three or four calls won't be as effective as the calls you'll make once your *are* warmed up.

So you make a spectacular flop of your first three calls of the day. What do you do then? You stop making calls, get yourself a cup of coffee, write a few letters and then maybe you make some tele-calls on softer, known customers who you feel will give you a better reception than the first three.

What have you done? You've blown the whole day.

How to Beat This

To be successful on the telephone every morning you are scheduled for tele-selling, get to work *early* – by 8.30 for the normal 9.00 start.

Don't listen to the news when you wake up. Don't read the newspaper. *All bad news.* You don't need it.

Get yourself some motivational audio tapes, sales related or the right, stimulating kind of music. Couple these into your wake-up call.

Begin each day with a good breakfast. Not necessarily a lot of food – just make sure it's good food.

Warm up on your own or with a colleague. Practise your word tracks across the office. Tape-record your calls and play them back for evaluation.

Make sure you are on top form when you get down to business and start telephoning your actual prospects.

Once you begin your tele-calls, *visualise* yourself succeeding. You Emotions are already warmed up and positive.

The Mirror in Your Front Hall

The next most important object in your home is the mirror on the wall of your front hall.

Before you step out of the door to begin your journey to the real work ...

Check yourself out in the hall mirror – head to foot. If you don't have a full-length mirror, get one quick. From your hair to your shoes, check that the image you are projecting is the one you want your customers to see.

Would *you* buy anything from someone who looks like that? If the answer is a resounding YES, then – well done, and off you go. If you feel the least bit dubious, then do something about it. Be honest about it. You know that white socks don't look right with black shoes, now don't you. And that *tie!!!*

LOOK GOOD,
FEEL GOOD.
LOOK SMART,
WORK SMART.

Your Greatest Asset

If someone offered you the world's most sophisticated computer to help run your business, you'd jump at the chance and feel pretty confident that it would enhance your performance, provided, of course, that you read the manual and worked out how to use it. Well, believe it or not, you already have that computer – it's called your mind – but the chances are you don't have a clue about how to make real use of it.

The real power of the mind is hidden in the subconscious. In fact, the subconscious controls about 90 per cent of what you do, including all your vital functions, while the conscious mind deals with the other 10 per cent, but getting to that critical 90 per cent is no easy matter.

You may think you've decided on a course of action, but if your subconscious isn't working with you, you'll keep finding apparently insurmountable problems in your way. You are programmed to fail. It may be that, deep down, you're afraid of succeeding; it may be that you don't actually believe that you deserve to succeed. Whatever the problem in your subconscious, you can feed in new information that will, in time, overcome these old-established negative attitudes and put you firmly on the track to success. It's simply a question of altering the programme of that amazing computer.

Success, happiness and achievement are all down to your state of mind! What happens in someone's physical world is simply a manifestation of the thoughts, attitudes and expectations of their inner world. After all, everything that you see about you which is man-made began as a thought in someone's mind. The reason that so many people don't get what they want from life is because they don't yet realise that all change and progress, both positive and negative, starts on the inside – in the mind – and works its way out into the physical world. The only difference between a person who's got it together and someone who hasn't is what goes on in their head. The exciting thing is that you can get inside there and change an awful lot of what goes on!

The Inner Game

If we are to be successful in the outer game, we must first learn the rules to play the **inner game**. To get to grips with this, we must understand the workings of our conscious and subconscious minds.

Our conscious mind is responsible for our current reality, our awareness of immediate events – the information we're absorbing now. When we try to do something with our conscious minds, it is described as 'thinking', 'decision making' and 'will power'. It is analytical – weighing up evidence to decide what is true and what is false, what is right and what wrong. The conscious is like an input/output device connected to the mainframe computer of the subconscious mind. It is really just the tip of the mental iceberg.

The subconscious mind is a very different animal. Unlike the conscious mind, which can really only deal properly with one thought at a time (did you ever try to listen to two conversations at once?), the subconscious runs any number of processes simultaneously. It is more powerful than the conscious mind by a factor of probably 10,000,000 to one and it runs all the time, even when the conscious mind is resting, during sleep. It stores every experience as a memory, although the vast majority of this information is unavailable to the conscious mind. It contains our beliefs, values and our self-concept – the software that makes us behave the way we do. It's our subconscious that drives us.

Part of our 'thinking' is our imagination. Imagination isn't just for kids, it's a very real part of us and to empower ourselves we must understand it and make it work for us. What you imagine, in terms of your inner dialogue, mental pictures, emotions and feelings, is taken on board as fact by your subconscious. Imagination is the information superhighway between your conscious and subconscious mind. Your subconscious will always triumph over your conscious will power, whether you want it to or not. So it makes sense to program your subconscious with the most positive images possible so that it can then set about transforming imagination into reality.

Your subconscious empowers you, at a subtle and fundamental level, to do the things necessary to transform your imagination into reality, perhaps even against your conscious will. It cannot distinguish between what is imagined and what is real. The key to personal empowerment is, therefore, learning to use your imagination to programme your subconscious mind.

The outcome of your actions is contained within the expectation. If you program your subconscious with the appropriate expectations, your actions will achieve what you want them to achieve. It's a simple as that.

Are you shaking you head in disbelief? Then here's some proof.

Parking Places Aplenty

Just try this. Next time you're going out in the car and you'll need a parking space, imagine yourself finding the space you want.

Try not to let your conscious mind interfere by starting to rationalise about it. Don't start telling yourself that you won't find a space and how hard it is. That's self-sabotage! Just relax and see yourself driving to where you want to go and there is a space for you. Use all your senses as you imagine it – see the space and feel the rightness and excitement as it appears just where you want. Just do it. I promise you it works! Let me explain why.

Because your subconscious holds the belief, based on past experiences, that parking spaces are as rare as rocking horse manure, you give up before you start even looking for one. You don't even really look. And so, of course, you don't find one – there you've been proved right again, and your subconscious belief is confirmed once again. How reassuring!

But when you show your subconscious exactly what you want, by using your imagination to give it a clear picture of how things are to be, without questioning how, you start a powerful process. What happens is that you engage your creative subconscious – the part of you that supplies you with ideas and inspiration.

A number of things will happen. Firstly, you'll find yourself driving down the street that most people have written off for parking – you'd have done exactly the same if you hadn't got your subconscious in on the act. Next, even if you don't see the space at first, at a level below your conscious awareness, you hear an engine starting up, you see a reversing light flash on, you see a puff of exhaust. These are the things your creative subconscious is on the look out for, so it can let you know that a space is becoming available – then you become consciously aware! And you go for it!

That's how we work. See what you want (not what you don't want) in your imagination as clearly as you can. See it, hear it, feel it, smell it, taste it. Don't question how you are going to achieve it. Allow your creative subconscious to go to work for you, to handle the details and to orchestrate the opportunities. All you have to do is be alert to opportunities to move you closer to your eventual goal.

Once you've proved to yourself that this works with a few simple examples, like parking, go a few steps further. In deepening your understanding of how this works, start to imagine your life the way you'd like it to be. Don't question how – that will only serve to limit your options and shut out your creative subconscious. If you use this visualisation process on a daily basis, I promise you can bring the things into your life that you once thought were out of reach. By using your imagination to program your subconscious as to how things are to be, you're able to influence situations that are well outside your current conscious realms of possibility. Don't ask how – just do it, and see the end result.

Your Self-image

Your self-image, sometimes also known as your Inner Mirror, is the way you see yourself – the kind of person you see yourself as being. This self-image is a combination of all the thoughts, experiences, concepts, ideas and events that have happened to you through your life, forming the composite picture of the person you see yourself to be.

Your self-image is made up of hundreds of self-concepts. You have a concept of what kind of manager, what kind of communicator or negotiator you are. You have self-concepts about your skill level at DIY, gardening and car mechanics, and you have self-concepts about your physical appearance, how likeable you are and how sociable. Basically, you have a self- concept for everything you are and do. And if you undertake a new task, before even starting it you will have a self-concept at the ready, based on the general view you have of your self-image. It will fit in with the way you see yourself, the level you pitch all your activities, even the level at which you have limited your aspirations.

Each self-concept is the governing factor in your performance in that area, because you will always perform in a manner consistent with that self-concept.

Your self-concept, therefore, precedes and predicts your performance and you will find it very difficult to perform in a way that contradicts your basic self-concept. Even if you do, you subconscious – whose job it is to maintain sanity by ensuring that you will always act in a manner that fits your view of yourself – will ensure that you return pretty quickly to the level of performance that agrees with your self- concept.

Let me give you an example:

Someone is playing golf. His self-concept as a golfer is average or below and he expects to get round the course OK but he might lose a few balls and make a few embarrassing shots in the process. On the third tee, he hits the ball perfectly and it flies up the fairway like a shot from a canon. 'Fantastic', he says, 'I don't usually play shots like those'. His next shot is equally good. The ball flies high into the air and drops on to the green. 'Can I do this? He says to himself. 'Can I really get it down in three?' With his goal in sight, he puts the ball straight into the hole.

The golfer is now a very happy and excited person because he has far exceeded his self-image as a golfer and thus his expectations. He walks quickly with great excitement and self-amazement to the next tee shot, wondering if could do this again. But alas no! His next shot is a big disappointment and he returns to his previous, rather lack-lustre form.

What has happened to him and to countless other people in comparable situations is that because his performance has surpassed and therefore conflicted with his self-concept as a golfer, he has become excited, and disbelieving of his achievement. His subconscious has brought his performance back in line with his self-concept. The role of the subconscious is to ensure that we always perform in a manner consistent with our self-concepts and self-image.

Had his self-concepts been higher and had he not become excited, the story would have been different. So because our self-concepts and self-image govern our performance in any given area, we must change our inner picture if we are to change our external performance. Expectation governs outcome.

Self-talk

Our subconscious listens to everything we say and acts blindly upon the information it receives. If we tell ourselves we have a bad memory for names, then we disempower the part of our mind that remembers names. So as long as we keep saying this, then we keep forgetting names.

Fortunately, it's possible to reverse the process, through positive self-talk. All day long we are not only speaking to other people, we are in regular communication with ourselves, too. It's estimated that we have some 50,000 thoughts per day. Our subconscious records each one.

If we persistently say to ourselves such negative comments as, 'I'm no good at this', 'I can't do that'. 'This will be awful', we are instructing our subconscious to make it so for us and to create a self-image of failure, disempowerment and negativity. If we do well at something and then announce, 'That was lucky', we are making sure that we won't be able to do it again.

Conversely, when we use positive self-talk to encourage, support and praise ourselves, we build up our self-image. This results in our positive statements becoming wonderfully self-fulfilling prophecies. The feedback this creates goes to helping us to improve our self-image and raise our expectation, achievements and satisfaction to a level we never before dreamt possible.

Positivity – the 'Yes You Can' Formula

If we are to grow and develop, we must take responsibility for our active role in creating and maintaining a positive self-image through positive self-talk. In a never ending spiral, reaching higher and higher in terms of achievement and happiness, **positive self-talk** leads to **positive self-image** leads to **enhanced performance** and so on.

Once again –

ATTITUDE DETERMINES ALTITUDE

Winning techniques for **positive self-talk** have been developed by psychologists the world over and, time and time again they have proved how well they work. To give it the technical name, this approach to positive thinking is called Neuro-Linguistic Programming. If you go about it systematically, as explained here, it will allow you to reprogram your mind for success and eliminate all the barriers you put up to prevent you achieving what you want in life. It is simply a question of developing and understanding the way your mind works and using that knowledge to your advantage.

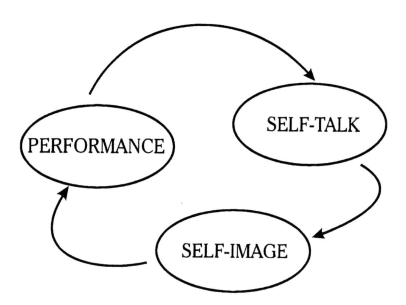

Programmed to Succeed

According to psychologists, most of the programmes in your subconscious are long established and, unfortunately, negative. It all starts in childhood, when adults are in such a hurry to tell you all the things you can't and shouldn't do that they forget to point out all the wonderful things you can do. And it's downhill from there. By the time you reach adulthood, your subconscious has probably become your own worst enemy. This is where Neuro-Linguistic Programming (NLP) comes into its own.

Try making a list of your goals and aspirations. Look at those now, and you will realise that the main obstacle between you and the achievements on that list are your subconscious negatives. Until you reprogram these, one at a time, you will continue to prevent yourself moving ahead and enjoying the benefits that achieving your goals will bring.

There's no time to lose. You have to start undoing a lifetime of negative thinking, but you *can* do it with NLP.

Putting it into Action

For NLP, all you need is some PRS. Don't panic – it's simpler than it sounds. PRS stands for positive reprogramming statements, which are affirmations you devise yourself to counteract your own weaknesses and fears. Only you know what your fears are and how you express them to yourself in your daily Self-talk.

This is going to be painful, but what you have to do now is to admit them to yourself as honestly as you can and write them down in a list. Here are some typical examples. See – you're not alone in this. Everyone has them.

Underline the ones that apply to you:

- I can't…
- I shouldn't…
- I'm going to fail…
- I'm unlucky…
- I'm always wrong…
- It's not for me…
- I'm too old…
- I've never been successful before, so how can I be now…?
- Nobody loves me…
- People will laugh at me…
- I'm not a likeable person…
- I can never seem to get my act together…
- I'm going bankrupt…
- I'm going to lose my job…
- My husband/wife is going to leave me…
- I'll always be unhappy…
- I'm going to be ill…
- I'm always tired…
- I'm neurotic…
- I'm shy…
- I don't know how to assert myself in public…
- Nobody pays any attention to me…
- I'll never get very far in life…
- I'm worthless…
- Success isn't in the cards for me…
- I was born under a bad sign…
- I'll never change…
- I can't plan my work…

- Nobody wants to buy anything from me...
- I'll never get out of debt...
- I'll never get promotion...
- I'm always getting up the boss's nose...

These become self-fulfilling prophecies. Do you notice something about all these negative statements. They are all excuses for giving up responsibility for what happens. They all express inevitability, with no possibility of improvement. No wonder they cast a shadow over people's lives. But it doesn't have to be like that.

On another piece of paper, write down the 'antidotes' to those poisoned statements, those negative beliefs about yourself. The important thing about them is that they should be:

positive;
progressive;
brief;
expressed in simple words;
each on one topic.

For example, if your negative is 'I'm too old to get this new job', reprogram it with 'I'm just the right age for this job', and so on. For 'I can't' substitute 'I can', for 'I always fail' substitute 'I will succeed'. Honestly, just reading them will make you feel better.

- I can...
- I should...
- I'm going to succeed...
- I am creating my own good luck...
- I am getting more and more things right...
- I can do anything I want...
- I'm just the right age...

- I have a wealth of useful experience that is helping me succeed…
- I love and I am loved…
- People are valuing me more and more for being my unique self, just as I value them…
- I can gain control of the way I organize my work…
- I can achieve greater prosperity…
- I can work effectively and successfully in any environment…
- My partner and I are growing closer to each other…
- Happiness is my right. I am happier and more contented every day…
- I am brimming with ever more health…
- My energy levels are increasing…
- I am becoming more calm and contended…
- With every passing day, I am becoming more confident…
- I radiate assurance and people are paying me more and more attention…
- People listen to what I have to say…
- I can achieve everything I dream of – and more…
- I am a unique and valuable person. I am special…
- Success is mine for the taking…
- Starting now, I can achieve anything I want to…
- I can change my old patterns. I have the determination to become better…
- I am gaining control of my work patterns…
- I inspire customers with confidence. I can help them solve their problems…
- I am clearing all debts and moving into increasing profit…

- My career is taking off. I am becoming more and more suitable for a higher position...
- I am showing my boss what an important part of the sales team I am. I am leading the way...

Once you've found and written down the antidotes for all your negative statements, take the negatives list, and say goodbye to it. Then tear it up, jump up and down on it, set fire to the pieces, put it through the shredder or just throw it away. You don't need it any more – it's a part of your past.

Moving Ahead to Success

Take one of the PRS on your list – choose the one you feel like working on first.

Let's say, for example, you decide on:

'I can complete all my paperwork, quickly and efficiently, every day'.

First write it down on a blank piece of paper. Nice big letters. Nice black ink. It's a bit like doing lines at school (maybe those teachers did know a thing or two!). INK IT AND THINK IT. Now read it out to yourself, clearly and confidently. It's important to read it out loud and not simply to think it, because it enters the mind in a different way and is processed by the subconscious more efficiently.

Repeat that statement to yourself at least 10 times a day (100 times a day would be more effective, but you have to get some work done as well), every day for three weeks. By then it should have worked its way into your subconscious and you can start work on another statement. To back this up, you can make a tape of yourself repeating your affirmation and play it to yourself in the car, but this time you would address yourself in the third person, saying 'You can complete all your paperwork, quickly and efficiently, every day'.

The benefits are immediate, but you probably won't be aware of them for some days. They accumulate with every repetition of your PRS, so remember, the more you do, the greater the effect. Gradually, you will banish the old, negative thoughts and beliefs that were holding you back and replace them with affirmations that will actually help you move towards your goals of self-development.

Just for fun, here are some more PRS, particularly suited to the profession of Selling. They make good motivational slogans too, so try sticking them on the wall where you and anyone else you want to motivate will see them:

WHAT I DO IS THE MOST EXCITING THING I CAN DO WITH MY CLOTHES ON

THERE ARE HUNDREDS OF OPPORTUNITIES OUT THERE

THERE ARE HUNDREDS OF PEOPLE OUT THERE WHO NEED WHAT I SELL

I CAN FIND THEM – I CAN MAKE THINGS HAPPEN

I CAN ACHIEVE ANYTHING I WANT TO ACHIEVE

I CAN PLAN MY WORK – I CAN WORK MY PLAN

I CAN INCREASE MY CUSTOMERS' SALES AND PROFITS

I CAN IMPROVE MY CUSTOMERS' CASH FLOW

I CAN REDUCE MY CUSTOMERS' COSTS

I CAN SAVE MY CUSTOMERS MONEY

I CAN HELP MY CUSTOMERS GAIN PRESTIGE AND MARKET SHARE

I KNOW I SELL THE BEST AND I KNOW HOW TO SHARE THIS KNOWLEDGE WITH MY CUSTOMERS

OUR PRICE IS A REFLECTION OF OUR QUALITY AND SERVICE

I GIVE VERY GOOD VALUE

NOBODY DOES IT BETTER

I CAN GET ORDERS ON THE TELEPHONE

I CAN EFFECTIVELY SERVICE MY EXISTING CUSTOMERS
ON THE TELEPHONE

MY CUSTOMERS CAN FIND ALL MY NEW BUSINESS FOR
ME – ALL I HAVE TO DO IT ASK THEM

I MUST SPREAD HAPPINESS

EVERY DAY IN EVERY WAY, I'M GETTING BETTER AND
BETTER

MY HEALTH AND ENERGY ARE IMPROVING DAILY.
TOMORROW I'LL WAKE UP IN GREAT SHAPE

I AM MORE AND MORE SUCCESSFUL IN EVERYTHING I DO

IF I DON'T CLOSE, I'M WORKING FOR THE COMPETITION

I CAN ASK FOR THE ORDER AND GET IT

FROM ME THE CUSTOMER GETS A COMPLETE PACKAGE –
AND THE MOST IMPORTANT PART OF THE PACKAGE IS ME

NOBODY DOES IT BETTER

So there you are. Don't leave good luck to chance – make every day your lucky day (and be much happier into the bargain) with the infallible 'Yes, You Can' formula, and leave the competition behind.

And remember:

The only difference between an
ACT
and a
HABIT
is
REPETITION

'We've got strengths and we've got weaknesses – but so have our competitors. If we sell our strengths against their weaknesses, we'll win.'

John Fenton

Chapter 4

How to Organise Yourself for Chasing Business, Not Just Customers

Most calls made by most salespeople are not *effective* calls because they lack an **objective** – a reason for the call which the customer or prospective customer himself sees as worth his time. With first-ever calls on new prospects, the reason for the call – the objective – will come straight from the carrot you dig up out of the research you do into the prospective customer's business, situation, aspirations and problems.

But for repeat calls on existing customers, or repeat calls on prospects, a call without an objective is the 'dreaded lurgie' of Selling. Such a call (especially if it is made out of the blue without a prior appointment) is called a **courtesy call** – and it often drives the customer mad.

The simplest kind of courtesy call goes like this:

> 'Morning George; how're things? Everything okay? Fine – see you next month, then. Bye!'

No research. No advance thought. No questions to probe for anything new that might be happening with the customer. No offer to tell the customer any news you've picked up which might be useful to him. Just routine – the old rut.

An interesting thing to remember if you *have* an objective is that *then* you are *chasing business, not chasing customers.*

If you ever look at trends in Selling – and I probably look at a lot more than most – you'll find that the more experienced salespeople get, the more they tend to throw away the Selling manual and play things off the seat of their pants.

Their *egos* take over and convince them that they don't need to do research, dig up carrots and make appointments any more, that their experience will carry them through. *It doesn't work.*

The result of this ego trip is that they probably stay just average salespeople, earning average money, never getting promoted.

Two epigrams fit this situation:

> 'Experience is not what happens to you – it's what you do with what happens to you.
>
> *Aldous Huxley*

> 'We judge ourselves by what we feel capable of doing, while others judge us by what we have already done.
>
> *Henry Wadsworth Longfellow*

Putting it into my words – ego is screwing up the will to *win*.

There is a second criteria for an effective call – a 'chasing business' call. You must get face-to-face with the right MAN – the key decision-maker who, to qualify for that title, must have three things going for him:

Money

Authority

Need

If the key decision-maker is a woman, it goes:

Wherewithal

Or

Money

Authority

Need

I find it incredible the number of salespeople I meet who don't know which customers and prospective customers they should concentrate on – those due for a 'chasing business with an objective' call – and which customers they can put aside for a while without risk. Both kinds are bundled together in their call plan.

Invariably this tells me that the salespeople in question are not properly organized. Also they're not doing enough research. They obviously don't really want to win, and they're hardly likely to win against any kind of professional competition.

Being properly organized, so as to make 100% effective calls, is, in fact, much *easier* than playing things off the seat of your pants. You see, effective calls derive from only five places:

- Customer records and prospective customer records
- Suspect lists
- Outstanding proposals lists
- Enquiries from advertising
- Customers who holler!

If you operate a record system that includes the first three of these five, plus facilities for dealing with the other two, you'll not only maximize your effective calls, you'll find it very easy indeed to put together a really meaningful weekly call plan – and that will please your sales manager no end. (Remember the Longfellow epigram?) And remember this – Any salespeople who don't keep their records religiously up-to-date and in apple-pie order are reducing their effectiveness and therefore are declaring themselves losers.

Customer and Prospective Customer Records

The best kind of Record is a foolscap-size manila *file,* not a card. With a file, for repeat business and prospective customers alike, all correspondence, copy action reports, quotations, drawings, can be kept safely *inside* the file. Everything in the one place.

A properly designed Record File, as illustrated in Chapter 2, properly used, brings many benefits to the successful competitive salesperson. For example:

- It facilitates efficient and longer-term planning of territory coverage (maximum calls, minimum miles).

- It increases the number of hours available for face-to-face selling (the selling day is *not* steadily getting shorter – this is only a myth, much promoted by bleating sheep)

- It banishes Courtesy calls forever (every call made has a clearly defined prior agreed objective).

- It minimizes Abortive calls (best day and time, appointment preferences, lunch habits, agreed call frequencies, etc.).

- It gains the salesperson advance commitment of a kind almost impossible to achieve by other methods (the 'Sales forecast' section).

- It enables the salesperson to use local third-party references during the sales presentation (the 'nearest other customers' section).

- The way the record file is filed away in the salesperson's system provides *automatic* sorting of which customers are due for a call at any point in time.

Maximizing Calls – Minimizing Mileage

The more the salesperson knows about his customers' and prospective customers' habits, the easier it is to achieve this objective. Consider the 'DMU Personnel' section in the record file. There is provision for eight key contacts, numbered 1-8, within the decision making unit. There is room to circle the code numbers of the most important contacts. There is provision for listing the full name, initials, job title and telephone extension of each contact.

Following this, there is detailed provision for listing each contact's habits:

Best day and time for a visit. Is he normally out on Mondays and in on Thursdays? Is he clear of clog before 10.00am because the post hasn't yet reached him? Does he work on after normal closing time? If so, will he see *you* after closing time (I assume, of course, you'll see *him!*).

Lunch habits. Does he go out, go home or eat sandwiches at his desk? If sandwiches, can you bring yours and join him during lunchtime to discuss that outstanding project?

DMU PERSONNEL	FULL NAME OR INITIALS	JOB TITLE	TEL EXT	BEST DAY AND TIME	LUNCH HABITS	AGREED CALL FREQUENCY	APPOINT OR P'CARD	BIRTH DAY	OBJECTIVE PRIORITIES
1									
2									
3									
4									
5									
6									
7									
8									

Agreed call frequency. How often do you need to call on each contact to be as certain as you can of securing the business that's available? Can you alternate a visit with a telephone call?

Appointment preferences. Does he insist on firm appointments every time, some of the time, or is he happy that you 'drop in' on the preferred day, at the preferred time and at the preferred frequency, without an appointment, sending him a 'reminder' postcard a week before? There is even room to make a note of his birthday, and his selected objective priorities.

Once you have all this 'habit' information agreed and documented on your record file, it is incredibly simple to maximize 'chasing business' calls and to minimize mileage. How do you get all that information? Well, dummy, you just *ask the contacts themselves.* Face-to-face, with that record file in your hot sticky hand. You write down the answers you get to your questions and you let them see clearly what you are doing.

Do you get the feeling you'll offend anyone? Of course not. You'll just come over to them as a more thorough, more professional salesperson. And that's what we're about!

Face-to-Face Selling Time

The average face-to-face Selling time for salespeople who take their products or services to the customers is probably running at less than two hours per day. That's no good at all. You must aim to double this if you want to win – to sell successfully against competition. We're halfway there already, with the 'DMU Personnel' information. To crack the other half, all we need to do is to make the Selling day longer.

In respect of the record file, this process begins with the defining of each customer's opening and closing times and the start and finish of his lunch break. You can have a special section on the file labelled 'Customer's Opening Hours' which is for this purpose. Without this fundamental information you don't really know where to begin. After that, it's entirely up to you. It's that Positive/Negative attitude thing again.

If you plan to get out of the metropolis before 3.30pm so as to avoid getting snarled up in the traffic, then, for you, the time you have for face-to-face Selling will be less, not more. Your success will follow the same trend.

If you don't use records like our example and you're prepared to be convinced that no customer will see you before 10.00am or after 4.30pm or between 12 noon and 2.30pm or on Friday afternoons, then there isn't much hope for you.

If you don't like getting up early, or if you get stuck with the school-kids' delivery and collection service, you've got big problems in this Selling business.

If you do anything deliberately to lower the number of days or hours you have available for Selling or for planning for Selling, you won't get far in this profession – and, worse than that, you're *stealing* from your employer. Time is money!

A true story: I know a sales manager with a great sense of humour who had a salesman suffering from a work problem – he didn't like it! This salesman was having one day off every two weeks with a migraine. Consistently. Too consistently!

The sales manager decided that the time had come to sort the salesman out. But he didn't want to demotivate him. No big sticks. No official warning letters. He simply called the salesman into his office one morning, sat him down across his desk and asked him to hold his hand out on the desk. Then he took a very large glass jar full of paracetamol tablets out of his desk drawer, unscrewed the top, and poured about 100 tablets into the salesman's outstretched hand. He put the jar down, closed the salesman's fingers round the tablets like a fist, held the fistful tightly, looked the salesman straight in the eye from 30 centimetres away and said:

'George, I don't care if you take these one at a time or all at once, you're not having a day off every two weeks with a migraine. Do I make myself clear?'

George muttered. 'Er, yes, I think so.'

'Off you go then,' said the sales manager, releasing the fistful of tablets. And off George went.

It cured his migraines. Don't know which way, but it cured 'em! And that's *brilliant* sales management.

Banish Courtesy Calls Forever

If you use the kind of record file we're discussing, then during every call you make on a customer or prospective customer you define and agree the objective for the next call.

That's why, in our example in Chapter 2, each line of the 'Call Record' is divided into two parts – 'What happened' and 'Objective for next call'.

And again, to maximize effectiveness and impact on the customers, both parts should be filled in while the salesperson is face-to-face with the customer, not back in the car.

Advance Commitment

This is the only bit of this book that deals with the much-neglected art of sales forecasting. You may produce weekly, or monthly or quarterly forecasts, best-bets lists, long-range predictions, market feels or whatever. It doesn't matter; the most important forecast is still the annual one.

But, if I may direct this next bit firmly towards management, the annual sales forecast, to be any use whatsoever, *must* be produced mainly by the people closest to the customers. The people at the sharp end, the salespeople. And a good annual sales forecast will take probably three months to produce. (If you give the salespeople three days, all you'll get is a wet thumb in the air!)

I say three months because this is the probable time it takes for a field salesperson to get round each and every one of the customers and known prospective customers in the territory – the Cycle Time. If your cycle time is different, substitute it for the three months.

During this three months, the salesperson is going about the normal worthwhile tasks, chasing business, making effective, non-courtesy calls. But during every call in this period, with the record file open at the ready, a couple of questions are added:

> 'I've been asked by my company to prepare a forecast of probable business for next year, Mr Jones. I wonder, could you give me any idea of what you are likely to be ordering from us in the next 12 months?' And referring to the record file, 'How does this relate to the business we've done so far this year and what we did last year?'

Consider carefully the very detailed kind of forecast you could produce if you had a 'Forecast' section in your record file. Not just total business in money terms. Also the spread over the year and broken down by product. Total calls required and how these are divided among the key contacts. An analysis of the competitors you

| | Calls on each key contact | | | | | | | | Total Calls | Total Business | Jan Mar | Business Spread Apr Jun |
	P	O	R	S	T	U	V	W				
FORECAST 19												
ACTUAL 19												
FORECAST 19												
ACTUAL 19												
FORECAST 19												
ACTUAL 19												

are up against in respect of this customer and how you are performing in relation to them.

Several hundred such precise forecasts, added together, produce the most accurate forecast any salesperson can arrive at. The most accurate because most of the data was provided *by the customers.* Some of these several hundred will be estimates made by the salesperson, of course; not every customer will co-operate fully. But even these estimates will be much more precise than that previous wet thumb in the air single guess for the total only.

Consider now what such a detailed forecast, contained as it is within the record file, means to the salesperson as the year of the forecast unfolds. Every time the salesperson pays a visit, he is monitoring the forecast given by the customer himself. If business falls behind the forecast, the salesperson can ask why, and will get a straight answer.

New Business Forecasts – the part of a salesperson's turnover that must come from prospective customers not even found at the time the forecast is produced – should be calculated jointly by management and the salesperson and be based on the salesperson's performance over the last three months and the new business target hoped for by the Company. For capital equipment salespeople, this might be as much as 80 per cent of the total forecast.

Here is an example:

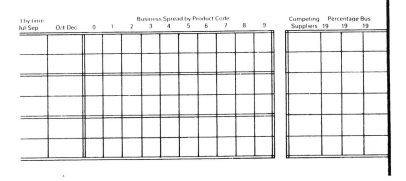

New business target – £400,000

Average order/account value in first year – £50,000

Number of new accounts required to achieve target:

400,000 ÷ 50,000 = 8 new accounts

Personal performance over past year ....
(count the types of calls – new business prospects only)

For every 5 first-ever-calls made, 1 proposal is submitted.

For every 5 proposals submitted on new prospects, 1 order is secured.

Thus, the number of first-ever-calls (new prospects) required to achieve new business target is:

8 x 5 x 5 = 200.

Assume there are 10 working months per year – that's 20 first-ever-calls per month.

Too many for comfort?

Okay, do something to improve your performance. That's what this book is all about. Say you could reduce those two ratios to 3 to 1 and 4 to 1 (see Chapter 5). How many new prospects would you need to find then?

8 x 3 x 4 = 96 or only 10 per month.

Local Third Party References

Back to our record file again and another section headed 'Nearest Other Customers'. This is important to the salesperson because, when he is establishing 'Best Day and Time' and 'Call Frequency' with any key contact, he also needs to remember which of his customers are nearby and on which days and at what times he calls on these customers. Then he can knit together the most effective day's work from the point of view of maximizing calls and minimizing mileage.

While doing this, he can show a prospective customer the list of nearby customers with whom he is doing business. A highly effective way of applying 'Joneses Principle' techniques.

Nearest other customers		
Name	Location	Best Day and Time for main decision makers

Automatic Sorting

Because every Next Call has a definite date and time (and failing this, an approximate date will do), with this kind of record file the normal method of filing away is *according to the date of the next call*.

The process is on-going. Every customer and prospective customer due for a call, say, in September will be there in the September slot, waiting for you, when September arrives. Or you can file by day, week or by month, whatever your business dictates. Self-adhesive colour codes are normally used at the top right hand corner of the record files (Area Code) to indicate the geographical location of the customer or prospective customer.

I have gone into some detail over these customer and prospective customer files, because it is the single most important, most powerful weapon in the professional salesperson's armoury. Learn to use it well, and success against the severest competition will be assured.

How One Salesperson Chases Repeat Business

I know of a car salesman who is not only a whizz at winning new customers (see *How to Win New Customers,* by John Fenton, published by Management Books 2000), he's also the guy who tries as hard as he can to *retain* his domestic customers once they've bought a car from him. He knows that, apart from fleet customers, he's unlikely to see a customer more than once every two years, unless something goes wrong, so the kind of customer record we've described is likely to be a trifle superfluous for his domestic customers. A simple card record is all he needs, on which he records date of sale, type of vehicle, requirements of customer and family, and, most important of all, *the date the hire purchase is due to be paid off,* if HP is involved.

In chronological order, the salesman does three things to try to retain his customer:

1. At the time of delivery of the sold car, he writes the ignition key number on the back of his business card, hands the card to the new owner and says:

    'Keep this card safe in your wallet/purse. I've written your ignition key number on the back, so if you ever lose your key, you'll be able to get another one without much bother.'

So, his business card stays with the new owner for the life of the vehicle, more often than not.

2. Three weeks *after* the new owner has taken delivery of the vehicle, and at six monthly intervals thereafter, the salesman telephones the customer, just to make sure everything is all right. Best time for this call is in the evening – the impression it makes is worth *extra* business, the customers tell their friends.

3. Two months *before* the hire purchase payments are completed, the salesman telephones the customer to establish what plans the customer has to dispose of the vehicle and acquire something new. The salesman has a demonstration ride all lined up, ready to offer. Then the cycle begins again.

It's so simple, why is it that 99 per cent of dealer salesmen *don't* do it?

Here's a letter used by Buick Motors, USA, in dealership sales training.

Dear Salesman:

I was surprised when you didn't see me a week or two after you delivered my new car that morning, not so many years ago, for I liked you and your company. I was planning on introducing you to some of my friends. I confess, I was a little disappointed when you didn't come. A good many times in the past years, especially for those first two when it was hard to find the payments on the car you sold me, I wished that you would come and tell me again about the values of it, and make me as enthusiastic about it as I was on the day whenI bought it... BUT YOU DIDN'T COME.

I was a little flattered when you persisted in seeing me, before I bought it. It made me feel worthwhile.! thought perhaps you liked me for my own sake as well as for the sake of my business. I thought you judged me an interesting fellow; but I guess I was mistaken for you never came back

Every year I think, well perhaps I should trade for a new car now, but then I spend more money on the old one and keep driving it. I have often wondered why you didn't come back to see me and save me that money... but you never came back. The man who sold me my first insurance policy likes me, and enough to come in to see me, even though he knows I don't need more insurance. The result is that I have been buying insurance from him all my life.! have spent a lot of money with your company ... more than I have buying insurance... BUT YOU NEVER CAME BACK.

Of course, I have bought lots and lots of cars from many different salesmen, each time thinking, 'I liked this man and will let him be my automobile salesman,' but my life has been a continuous procession of strange salesmen ... because THE OLD ONES NEVER CAME BACK.

Sincerely,
NEW CAR BUYER.

It says it all, doesn't it?

Suspect/Prospect Lists

The traditional way for salespeople to note down suspects and prospects as they come across them is on the back of cigarette packets or business cards. The snag is, half the notes are lost well before action can be taken on them. A more disciplined approach to self-generated and to company-generated prospecting is called for if you want to win – like the example suspect list overleaf.

REF. SL51266

"SUSPECT" LIST	AREA W. MIDLANDS	SALESMAN J. WATSON		
COMPANY NAME & ADDRESS	DECISION MAKER	POTENTIAL	BEST LINE OF ACTION & REASON	
Date 13/7 Source FACTORY EQUIP. NEWS — I.B.E. BIRMINGHAM 33 — Tel. No. 021-998-7061	R.J. JURY WORKS MANAGER	500 HBV UNITS.	DEMO 47B MODEL.	Card ✓ File Dead
Date 13/7 Source F.E.N. — SMITH DAVIDSON LTD BIRMINGHAM 6 — Tel. No. 021-978-8181	B. JONES DIRECTOR	BUYING 100 AJS FROM BIB PER YEAR.	TRY 47B FOR COMPARISON.	Card ✓ File Dead
Date 17/8 Source REFERRAL — MALTBY & PALMER COVENTRY — Tel. No. 0203-781880		QUOTING FOR SEWAGE WORKS.	CHECK PLANNING REGISTER FOR WORKS DETAILS.	Card File ✓ Dead
Date 18/8 Source LOCAL AD. IN TIMES. — VICTORIA FORGE BINLEY WOODS COVENTRY — Tel. No. 0203-347221	J. BRIDE BUYER	USE SNOOKS	HAVE DELIVERY PROBLEMS.	Card File ✓ Dead
Date 20/8 Source REFERRAL — TAYLOR & FLETCHER SMETHWICK — Tel. No. 021-493-4281	F. HARRISON PRODⁿ MGR.	MAKE M.O.D. COMPONENTS	CHECK SPEC-V-U84 FOR BETTER DEAL	Card ✓ File Dead
Date 27/8 Source ENG. DIGEST — TENSILE STEEL CO. CASTLE HILL DUDLEY — Tel. No. 0384-92631	H. WATKINS DEV. ENG		DESIGNING NEW PRESSURE SYSTEM	Card ✓ File Dead
Date 28/8 Source CHAMBER OF COMM. — C & F TOOLS LTD. BIRMINGHAM 10 — Tel. No. 021-776-3254	F. COCHRANE MAN. DIR.	HAS A RUSSIAN CONTRACT FOR 24 MKS	FIND OUT HYDRAULIC SPEC	Card File ✓ Dead
Date Source — Tel. No.				Card File Dead
Date Source — Tel. No.				Card File Dead
Date Source — Tel. No.				Card File Dead

© SALES CONTROL & RECORD SYSTEMS LTD. CONCORDE HOUSE, 24 WARWICK NEW ROAD, ROYAL LEAMINGTON SPA CV32 5JH

A 'Suspect' is someone, or some company, who just might be needing your products or services. A nibble, a name worth checking out. Detective fashion.

A 'Prospect' is a Suspect who's been checked out, and has come up positive. A carrot has been established. A potential has been estimated. The best line of attack and the reason for this line has been thought out and documented. The decision-maker has been pin-pointed. Everything is ready for the telephone call to make the first appointment.

The Suspect List illustrated is designed to take both self-generated suspects and suspects picked up by your company's advertising and sales promotion efforts. Some suspects also pop up out of the blue, telephoning your office and asking about something. The space labelled 'Source' is to indicate where the suspect came from.

The tick boxes labelled 'Card', 'File' and 'Dead' are for resultant action – you have made out a record card for this prospect (you don't consider he's worth a file yet!) or a record file (he looks very promising!) or you've written him off as useless. If you completely filled one of these Suspect Lists each month, and fully researched every new suspect to establish 'Best Line of Action and Reason' (the carrot!) before attempting to make the first appointment, you'd be well on the way to achieving a new business target based on 10 first-ever-calls each month. If your success rate of telephone calls to appointments was two to one, you'd need two such lists per month.

After your Suspect/Prospect lists have been completed and you have no further action to take on any name listed, you *never* throw them away. They either go back to head office for analysis of the sources of the names (how effective is your company's sales promotion, advertising and direct mail activity?) or you keep them yourself in an 'In Memoriam' file (dead but not forgotten).

Why? Because you may get promoted next year and find yourself supervising a novice salesperson doing the job you used to do. Do you want him to waste time chasing the *same* suspects you've already written off? And a dead suspect today might be a live prospect next year if your company brings out a new product.

Outstanding Proposals List

If you use the record files I've described, you'll rarely lose sight of an outstanding proposal that needs following up. The copy proposal is *in* the record file and the file is in the correct slot for your follow-up, if this is the most imminent action in respect of this customer.

If you use record cards instead of files, you cannot be this efficient. Your copy proposals need to be stored elsewhere, and with so little room on the record card to write anything really meaningful, there is always the danger of mislaying or overlooking a follow-up and and losing the business to a competitor. The 'Outstanding Proposals' sheet illustrated opposite is an effective way to solve this problem.

It has two sections, one for existing customers, the other for prospects, three columns in each section for dates of follow-up calls, and is designed to be used like a cash book, with ongoing entries as they happen. Proposals that result in orders or that you lose to competitors are struck out. Likewise, if you are asked by a customer to re-submit because of changes, the original proposal line is struck out, 're-submit' entered in the result column, and the re-submitted proposal itself becomes a new entry further down.

The 'Outstanding Proposals' list is also superb as a 'Best Bets' list for short-term forecasting, as it tells you the total business you've got in the pipeline at any point in time. Some Salespeople who use the list for this purpose use the follow-up columns to note important future dates – such as 'one week before decision day' or 'expected order placing day'.

OUTSTANDING PROPOSALS						SALESMAN J. WATSON					
E = EXISTING CUSTOMERS						P = PROSPECT					
DATE REQUESTED	DATE ISSUED	E OR P	QUOTE NO.	VALUE	COMPANY	PRODUCT GROUPS	FOLLOW UP 1 2 3 4 5				NEXT
2.8.82	4.8.82	E	7251	368	SIEMENS	9 & 10	4/9				O
2.8.82	6.8.82	E	7255	1021	JONES & STEEL	1 & 6	2/9 29/9 6/9				L
5.8.82	11.8.82	E	7259	481	POMEROY & CO	2	16/9 7/9				
10.8.82	24.8.82	E	7301	1671	EXEL VENTS	9 & 10	9/9				
20.8.12	29.8.82	E	7310	896	ASH & CO LTD	3	21/9				23
25.8.82	30.8.82	E	7311	184	ABRAHAMS	4	16/9 2/9				
2.9.82	9.9.82	E	7320	267	BREEDON SMITH	1					O
7.9.82	15.9.82	E	7351	900	P.K. VALVES	6	24/9 13/9				9/10
9.9.82	16.9.82	E	7363	1021	C & S	9 & 10	24/9				
21.9.82	29.9.82	E	7400	860	BLOGGS PUMPS	3	9/10				
30.9.82	2.10.82	E	7401	290	NORTONS	4	14/10				
25.10.82	26.10.82	E	7410	765	P.K. VALVES	9					
2.8.82	4.8.82	P	7253	496	E. GRAY & CO.	3	17/9				L
2.8.82	5.8.82	P	7254	870	ASTON HYD.	9	18/9				O
4.8.82	7.8.82	P	7256	488	A.P.T. LTD.	2	4/9 7/9				
11.8.82	20.8.82	P	7271	1066	DROP FORGES	1	9/9				O
20.8.82	21.8.82	P	7273	1290	DROP FORGES	1 & 6	9/9 9/9				
3.9.82	8.9.82	P	7333	440	HEREFORDS	4	22/9				O
6.9.82	10.9.82	P	7326	600	C. RIGBY	9	13/10				
12.9.82	18.9.82	P	7391	550	T. STEEL & CO.	1 & 3	9/10				
1.10.82	6.10.82	P	7402	413	SNOOKS ENG.	4	14/10				
7.10.82	18.10.82	P	7403	1030	ARNOLDS	4					
8.10.82	12.10.82	P	7409	460	WILD BROS.	3					

Following up Advertising Enquiries

Any enquiry generated by your company's advertising and sales promotion campaigns must be immediately followed up *by telephone*. Don't send literature and a covering letter. If you do,

---

Enquiry Follow-up by Telephone

1. Identify you are speaking to the Enquirer.
   "IS THAT MR. SMITH?"

2. Tell him who you are.
   "GOOD MORNING. MY NAME IS _____ OF _____ "

3. Set the scene for him to tell you why he enquired in the first place – and make sure you get the words EXACTLY right.
   "THANK YOU FOR ENQUIRING ABOUT OUR _____ "
   (or "thank you for sending in the coupon from our advertisement in _____ .)
   I'VE GOT A LOT OF INFORMATION I CAN SEND YOU, BUT JUST TO MAKE SURE I SEND YOU EXACTLY WHAT YOU WANT... TELL ME... WHAT MADE YOU ENQUIRE?"

4. Shut up – and write down here what he says.
   _____
   _____
   _____

5. Now all you have to do is ask him a few questions, relevant to the above reason for his enquiry – questions which will help you quickly decide if he is worth visiting or not; and questions which will also keep him turned on and impressed by your professionalism. Questions like:–
   "WHERE DO YOU BUY YOUR _____ FROM AT PRESENT?"
   _____
   "WHAT ARE YOU PAYING FOR _____ AT PRESENT?"
   _____
   "HOW MUCH OF IT DO YOU USE?"
   _____
   "WHAT HAVE YOU DONE SO FAR TO COPE WITH THIS?"
   _____
   "WHO ELSE ARE YOU IN TOUCH WITH?"
   _____

6. If you decide from this that a visit is warranted, finish like this:–
   "WELL, I CERTAINLY THINK WE CAN HELP YOU. LOOK, I'VE GOT SOME SAMPLES AND INFO ON A COUPLE OF OTHER COMPANIES LIKE YOURS WHICH I'D LIKE YOU TO SEE. I'M IN YOUR AREA... LET'S SEE... (consult diary)... NEXT _____ ; CAN YOU SPARE ME HALF AN HOUR SAY, AT _____ , OR WOULD _____ BE MORE CONVENIENT?"

   Appointment booked for _____

7. If you decide he's not worth a visit – send him something by post, and staple your business card to the top. It won't need a covering letter; just say:–
   "WILL IT BE OKAY IF I SEND YOU THE INFORMATION WITH MY BUSINESS CARD, RATHER THAN WITH A COVERING LETTER? I CAN GET IT TO YOU A BIT QUICKER THAT WAY."

---

when you follow up later, in the majority of cases all you'll get will be 'Ah, yes, we've received your literature. Nothing's going to happen for quite a while yet. When it does, we'll let you know.' You won't even find out the most important thing of all – *why he took the trouble to respond to your advertisement*. Without knowing this, you can't start selling.

Telephone first, preferably the salesperson who is going to do the selling. If this is not practical for some reason, use someone competent at head office or regional office. And *always* use a checklist. There is absolutely no excuse for getting anything wrong with this kind of telephone call. An example checklist is set out above. Section 3 is the most critical. You have to get that bit *exactly* right, or it won't work and you'll lose probably 30 per cent of the appointments you go for.

Making Appointments

With your customer record files, your suspect/prospect lists, your outstanding proposals list and your enquiry follow-up checklists, you have organized nearly everything you need for success. Nearly everything. You're still short of a mounted map of your territory, on which the precise position of each of your customers and known prospective customers is clearly indicated with a coloured map pin. And you need a decent sized diary. (You think I'm being just a touch too basic? Even patronising? You'll never convince me. I'm the guy who regularly addresses 2,000 Salespeople for a day and finds 400 of them have turned up without anything to write with, let alone anything to write on. Mounted maps and pins are just about unknown. Diaries not quite so bad.)

Assuming you have organized your map, pin-pointing all your known customers and prospective customers, you could still do with one more thing before you begin making appointments and building your weekly call plan – a piece of thin string.

So you know already the actual customers you want to call on next Wednesday. You know there are six of them. You know where they are situated. You know your start and finish point for the day. But, do you know the most economical order in which to call on these six customers? The route from one to the next through the day, which will result in the minimum of miles travelled? That's where the piece of string comes in. From home base, round the six pins denoting the six customers you want to call on, back to home base. Both ends held firmly in left and right hands. Off the pins on to a

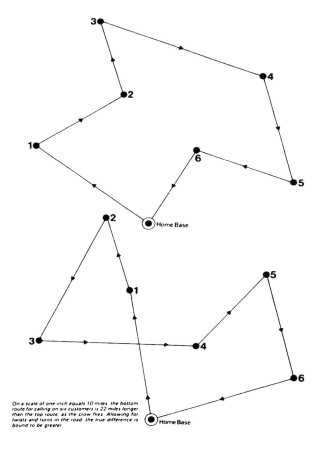

On a scale of one inch equals 10 miles, the bottom route for calling on six customers is 22 miles longer than the top route, as the crow flies. Allowing for twists and turns in the road, the true difference is bound to be greater

110

straight scale. Then try again another way round the six pins. And again. The shortest distance wins, and now you have two chances of achieving maximum calls in minimum miles travelled with this shortest distance – clockwise or anti-clockwise. You can extend this technique for territory planning, too, and this is dealt with in greater detail in Chapter 5.

Now you are ready to pick up the telephone and make some appointments. And just in case your ego is telling you not to bother with that daft idea with the piece of string, let me confirm that you'll still get the same number of appointments without it, more or less, but you'll finish the year having travelled maybe 5,000 miles further than you need have done and you'll have deprived yourself of the opportunity to use that travelling time to make maybe 250 extra calls. It's that simple.

Priority is for Prospects

Because first impressions count for a hell of a lot in this business, all your first-ever calls should be by appointment. Whether the prospective customer is self-generated or came by way of the advertising and sales promotion campaign, your initial research will have indicated the probable likely carrot to dangle. So hit him as professionally and as confidently as you can. Don't ever aim your first appointment of the day for mid-morning or mid-afternoon. The most effective aiming sequence for a day's appointment making is:

    First Appointment: 8.50am
    Second Appointment: 4.50pm (or 5.50)
    Third Appointment: 11.50am
    Fourth Appointment: 1.50pm
    Fifth Appointment: 9.50am
    Sixth Appointment: 10.50am
    Seventh Appointment: 2.50pm
    Eighth Appointment: 3.50pm

If you make less calls a day, knock out the fifth to eighth. Keep the first to fourth.

Why the ten minutes to the hour timing? It's an interesting piece of applied psychology.

Most prospective customers who are telephoned by salespeople have a subconscious clock that tells them how much of their valuable time the salesperson is likely to need. Prospective customers' secretaries also have this subconscious clock.

If a salesperson telephones and suggest 'How about 11.00 am?' the subconscious clock journeys round from 11 to the next 12 o'clock and a voice in his brain tells the prospective customer; 'Hey, this salesperson is going to take an hour of my time'. That's too much of his time so he says 'No'.

Subconscious clocks all travel round to the next 12 o'clock. So an appointment suggested for 10.30 gets a half an hour reading. That's why appointments should be made at *ten to the hour*. Then they get a 10-minute reading and you have the best chance of getting a 'Yes'.

On 6 October 1982, I led a Road Show at Southampton, at which I explained this bit of psychology. On 8 October I received a letter from a Mrs Raie Balloqui, a director of a company selling business machines and electronic typewriters. She had been present at the Road Show. The letter read:

> Dear Mr Fenton,
>   I simply had to write and tell you ... from seven phone calls made this morning, I have six appointments booked for next week, all at 10 minutes to the hour!

Proof of the pudding...?

Writing or Telephoning 'Cold' for an Appointment

Prospects whom you find yourself are known as 'Cold' – the prospect himself has no idea you are about to descend upon him, and (you must assume) knows little or nothing about your company or your products or services. (Don't get this mixed up with Cold Canvass – that's something different.)

You may have dug up a suitable carrot, but this still has to be effectively dangled in front of the decision-maker's nose before he grants you the opportunity to get face-to-face.

You can dangle the carrot either by telephone or by letter.

Whether you choose to telephone or write, always remember that your objective is simply to secure an appointment – *not* to get involved in a detailed explanation of what you want to talk to him about *when* you get face-to-face. To avoid this problem, many good salespeople send a letter first and then follow up with a telephone call a few days later, aiming to reach the decision-maker's secretary who should know about the letter and be more receptive to the telephone call.

Here is an example letter for a fairly technical selling situation designed to be sent to the managing director or the production director of a prospect company.

> *Dear Mr Jones*
>
> *Technological advancement within your particular Industry is constantly bringing pressure to bear on companies, making them advance in step with technology or risk losing their share of the market.*
>
> *An additional problem is that the economic state of industry in general this year does not encourage companies to invest in the necessary new plant, yet to stay competitive they must do something.*

This is a problem on which my company has done a great deal of research and development. As a result, we have produced equipment, which for an extremely low capital investment, can increase automatic component production by something like 20 per cent over conventional methods.

If you can spare me an hour of your time, I would very much like to show you exactly what we have done at other firms similar in size to your own and discuss how our equipment might be of benefit to you.

May I telephone your secretary on Friday to fix a definite appointment?

Yours sincerely

John Fenton

Midlands Representative

The carrot you are dangling has to be very obvious. There are two carrots in this example letter:

1. Increase the prospective customer's component production by 20 per cent.

2. Show the prospective customer what you have done for other firms – maybe competitors, providing you do not betray any confidences.

Carrot 2 will be more powerful than carrot 1.

The managing director's curiosity will win the day almost every time.

Here are a few more choice phrases that are good for these kinds of letters;

*   '... you will save around 15 per cent of your monthly distributing costs.'

*   '... in less than ten minutes I can show you five ways for you to reduce your transport costs.'

- '... you can improve your productivity by at least 16 per cent – with less demand on men and machinery.'
- '... the enclosed article from Sludge Shifters Monthly explains what I am suggesting we can do for you.'
- '... why not telephone Mr Andrews of Bloggs Pumps Ltd and ask him what he thinks about us?'
- '... your neighbours, Snooks Engineering Ltd, have been using our model 47B very successfully for two years now.'

Next, here is an example from the Financial Services Industry, where it is probably more difficult to get face-to-face 'cold' than anywhere else.

Dear Mr Rowbottom

Would you mind letting me have your date of birth below so that I can provide you with detailed information on a new executive protection plan which, due to its low cost and high benefits, is probably the most talked-about policy in the financial services world today.

A stamped addressed envelope is enclosed for your convenience.

Very truly yours
John Fenton
Managing Director

Name _____

*Address*_____

Telephone Number _____ *Date of Birth* _____

The stamped addressed envelope *must* have a stamp, not be a printed reply-paid format. And, of course, the detailed information is not sent; the salesperson or the managing director (who will undoubtedly still be selling hard in this business) will telephone Mr

Rowbottom immediately on receipt of the returned letter and ask for an appointment, because there are a number of questions he still needs to ask and he's got some data on how other executives have done very well out of this new plan, which he feels Mr Rowbottom should see.

Going for the Very Top

The best example of writing for an appointment I have ever seen happened early in 1983, and may well go down in selling history as a classic for maximum 'knock-on' effect. The selling company in question was selling strong to many executives in many branches of the prospect company for many months, on the strength of just two letters they received in reply. With the permission of the perpetrator, here is the example in detail.

The company wrote, enclosing a sample of the product, to the Chairman of the British Steel Corporation. The covering letter read:

Mr I. MacGregor   *7 January 1983*
Chairman
British Steel Corporation
9 Albert Embankment
London, SEI

Dear Mr MacGregor
    Please accept a small aid to productivity.
    It is a spray nozzle that mounts and aligns in one movement. No screwing. No spanners. Repeated very often, and multiplied by thousands as sprays on big installations need cleaning or replacing, its simplicity could save a lot of maintenance time for the Steel Industry and safeguard product quality by making a necessary service task less liable to neglect.

The concept is new and unique and because we believe that it really can contribute to productivity at British Steel, we decided to be brave and go to the top. Anyone you referred us to would have our instant attention.
Yours sincerely

The reply from Ian MacGregor was dated 10 January 1983.

Dear Mr ...
Thank you for sending me a sample of your development of a new type of two-piece nozzle installation with a bayonet connection.
I have passed the sample on to Dr Fitzgerald, who heads our Technical and Engineering function, with a request that he evaluates the potentialities of the product and communicates with you directly.
Thank you for bringing this development to our attention.
Sincerely,

The selling company promptly made contact with Dr Fitzgerald, to make sure he had safely received the sample spray nozzle from Mr MacGregor. They also sent Dr Fitzgerald some technical information and performance data.

On 21 January 1983, a reply was sent to the selling company by Dr Fitzgerald.

Dear Mr ...
Thank you for your letter of 17 January. I have passed the information you sent me to our engineers. As soon as I have some response we will get together and discuss opportunities.
Yours sincerely

Now, at the time, the very vastness of the British Steel Corporation hid layer upon layer of inter-departmental politics, a

'Parkinson's Law' rivalry that created incredible quantities of obstacles which got in the way of progress. A rather cruel joke on this subject went – 'What's the difference between the British Steel Corporation and British Rail? Answer – the British Steel Corporation carries more passengers!'

The new and unique spray nozzle, if sold to the maintenance engineering department of, say, Port Talbot works, might be tried out and a few dozen subsequently ordered, but that would be as far as things would go. The last thing likely to happen would be for someone to recommend the nozzle to another British Steel works.

By starting at the very top, this selling company had bypassed the politics, but in such a way that, from then on, the normal obstacles at works level were replaced with politically motivated enthusiasm. The salesforce of the selling company were busy all over the UK, at all levels of BSC. Wherever they went, whoever they talked to, copies of the two letters from Ian MacGregor and Frank Fitzgerald went with them. Maintenance engineers, works engineers, plant managers, divisional directors competed frantically to make it known to the top brass that they supported this new development. Response was what Dr Fitzgerald had said he was waiting for. Response was certainly what he got.

A very effective way to secure a 'Cold' appointment by telephone is for a salesman to use his wife, or an office-based secretary, to make his appointments for him. If he uses his wife, the kids and all domestic background noises must be banished. This is absolutely essential. The wife, when she telephones prospects, is *never* the salesman's wife – she is *always* his secretary. The call goes like this:

'My boss, Mr Andrews, has asked me to telephone you to arrange for him to come and see you – hopefully some time next week. I think it is in connection with improvements in your widget crushing plant. Could you spare Mr Andrews ten

> minutes, er, on Tuesday next, say at 9.50, or would the afternoon be better for you, say 10 minutes to three?'

Often the prospect plays hard to get and asks for more information. This is where having a secretary who telephones is a winner:

> 'I'm terribly sorry, but I don't know any more. Mr Andrews just asked me to make the appointment. Look, if Tuesday is not convenient for you, would Wednesday be better?'

Alternative choice of date and times, always.

Ladies take on a dual role for appointment making. They become their own secretaries.

The most difficult people to get face-to-face with 'Cold' are people like architects. They tend to hate salespeople. They don't like sales literature much either. So unless they have a specific need for something, the answer nine times out of 10 is 'No, go away!'

One company I know cracked this problem with ease. They harnessed the one factor that *did* turn architects on – *innovation*. Architects are designers, first and last. They yearn to create something that will make a name for themselves, win a building prize, enable them, if they work for a large firm, to set up in practice for themselves.

So whereas architects dislike sales literature, they simply *love* design manuals. This company therefore took their standard brochure on the products, which happened to be a range of mechanical and hydraulic dock levellers for warehouse loading bays, added some extra pages at the front on how to design loading bays which used their dock levellers, and retitled the brochure *'Modern Loading Bay Design'*.

The company's salespeople then telephoned architects and said:

'We've brought out a new design manual for loading bays. I'm in your area next Tuesday, can I drop you a copy in and show you the recent developments we've put into it?'

Success rate increased from one out of 10 to six out of 10.

Incoming Telephone Calls

You don't have to telephone every prospect. Sometimes they telephone *you,* but when they do, there is still your back-up to contend with.

Many a hot prospect has been lost because his telephone call was badly handled when he made the first contact, out of the blue. His requirements were not listened to or properly documented. The note made got lost before it could be sent to the salesperson in the territory. The voice he heard irritated or depressed him.

No one can afford to lose business in this kind of way. Set out opposite is a specially designed Action Report for Incoming Telephone Calls.

There are two essential rules for the use of this form:

1. The person in your office who is going to pick up the telephone when it rings has a pad of these forms, and writes his/her full name on each sheet of the pad before business begins for the day. This simple action doesn't just make sure that the person taking the telephone call can be identified after the event it also gets the person accustomed to using his/her full name when the phone rings – 'Good morning, Sally Haynes, how can I help you?' (It's incredible how reluctant people can be about using their own names.)

Incoming Telephone Call   Action Report

It's ringing... but before
you pick up the phone

**"Good Morning
Good Afternoon**

(say christian name and surname)

Can I help you?"

Person taking the call must fill in his/her name

SMILE!

(go on, force yourself)

Date of call _____ Time of call _____

Name and Initials of Caller _____
(ask him/her to spell name if in doubt)

Company (if relevant) _____

Address (if relevant) _____

_____ Post Code _____

Telephone Number (if relevant) _____ Extension _____

Reason for the Call _____

_____

_____

_____

_____

_____

Action to be taken agreed with caller _____

_____

_____

_____

_____

The Institute of Sales & Marketing Management

---

2. Before the ringing telephone is picked up, the corners of the person's mouth *must* be turned upwards – he/she *must* be smiling. A mirror on the desk helps. 'Think a smile' is a fundamental rule throughout Selling. It's a physiological fact that when your face is smiling your voice comes out happy. Even on black days when you feel like death warmed up, when you grit your teeth and force yourself to smile, your voice will still come out happy. The mirror on the desk is really for the black days. You grit your teeth, look in the mirror and force yourself to smile. It looks so darn stupid to you that you start laughing. So pick up the phone – 'Good morning, Sally Haynes, how can I help you?'

Customers who Holler

The few customers who holler for you to go and *see* them, shouldn't be allowed to disrupt your plan. Don't drop everything unless it's a real emergency. Don't accept on face value the message passed to you by your office, either. Phone the customer back before you jump into your car. Make the visit on your terms – a day or two rarely makes any difference, it's just a misplaced sense of urgency building up in your mind. The better your planning, the easier it is to crack this problem.

The Resulting Call Plan

From the foregoing you can really get your teeth into making effective appointments, beating your competitors to the business that's going, making the customers prefer to do business with you rather than with some less professional, less organized, competitor's salesperson.

And from all this you'll be able to produce a proper, fully detailed call plan like the one illustrated below:

	TIME	APPT or COLD	COMPANY	CONTACT	TELEPHONE NUMBER	AIM OF CALL
MONDAY	8.50	A	PRESSED STEEL CO	J. BLACK	021-221 1961	GAIN ORDER
	11.30	C	POTTERSBY & CO	MAN DIR		FACTORY EXT. PLANNED
	2.00	C	J & B ENGINEERS	E. JONES		RE STOCK ORDER
	3.45	A	HEREFORD & CO	R. JUDSON	021-888 6464	NEG. CONTRACT RENEWAL FOR VALVES
TUESDAY	8.50	C	BAYTON ROAD, EXHALL — COLD CANVAS IND. ESTATE			
	10.50	A	FISHER & WADE	E. SAMSON	0203-88771	ENQ FOR PUMPS
	2.00	C	CONTINUE COLD CANVAS			
	3.50	A	EXHALL TOOLS	R. FRANKS	0203-07681	DISCUSS NEW VALVE
WEDNESDAY	9.00	A	MEET SALES MGR @ COVENTRY STATION			
	9.50	A	JONES & PLAT	N. SMYTHE	0203-38221	NEW CONTRACT FOR VALVE
	1.50	A	DROP FORGES	J. HINKLEY	0203-47681	GAIN ORDER
	2.50	A	F. LACEY & CO	L. BRIGGS	0203-43255	DISCUSS NEW VALVE
	3.50	A	ARUNDEL DEVELOPMENT DIRECTOR WORKS			BUILDING NEW WKS
THURSDAY	8.30	A	ALL DAY @ H.Q. PRODUCT TRAINING ON NEW VALVE.			
FRIDAY	9.50	A	B.S.C.	M. DALY	COSBY 57221	COMM. NEW PLANT
	11.50	A	AQUASCUTUM	R. ROSS	COSBY 56655	GAIN ORDER
	2.00	A	BRITISH SEALED BEAMS	D. DAVIES	COSBY 58241	DISCUSS NEW VALVE
	3.50	A	GOLDEN WONDER	N. JENKS	COSBY 59911	INCREASE STOCKS

CALL PLAN   WEEK NO 14   SALESMAN J. WATSON

One of the oldest formulae for success in Selling comes to mind here. It goes:

PLAN YOUR WORK   WORK YOUR PLAN

That's how to make sure you're always chasing business, not just chasing customers or will-o'-the-wisps. Common sense? Of course it is. But as I've said before common sense isn't practised all that often in Selling – unless you really want to win, that is!

Break a Leg!

The telephone is a most under-utilized Selling tool, except in businesses like Birds Eye, Ross Foods and Coca-Cola, where it gets 95% of total business when used by Tele-Sales teams.

Most salespeople traditionally believe that the customers much prefer the face-to-face approach. One salesman I know proved it was all different. He didn't set out to prove it – he just broke his leg in seven places, skiing, and wound up in traction for six months without the option.

Lying there, he began worrying about his customers, and about his job. (Wouldn't you?) So he resolved to do something about it. He got his wife to collect together all his customer records, files, cards, assorted paperwork and deliver it to his bed Then he set about devising a plan for systematically telephoning every one of his customers and prospects, potential business determining the frequency of the phone call. One of his colleagues handled any trouble-shooting necessary during the six months.

And what did he find?

Business didn't go down, it went *up!* Okay, during the first month he got a fair bit of sympathy business and, not being a dummy, he took advantage of this, but after the initial month, business still kept increasing. The salesman himself told me why, a few months after he'd recovered and gone back on the road.

'I found I was contacting every single one of my customers about four times as frequently as when I was making visits to them. And, you know, they didn't mind. They didn't bother that it was just a telephone call, not a visit. They were quite happy doing business over the phone. This was the shock I had to get over. Okay, I had no other options open to me so I probably did a much better job on my phone calls than I would have done normally. But, it showed me the true situation.

'Now I spend only half my total time on the road, most of it chasing new business, and the other half manning my own Tele-Sales Desk. And sales are still going up.'

Maybe your business is different – but is it *that* different?

A Final Word on Paperwork

Most salespeople don't like it. Some positively hate it. Some go to great lengths to avoid it. One sales manager I know said this to me recently:

'One of my salesmen is allergic to NCR paper!'

Another sales manager I know received a formal doctor's note from one of his salesmen, which read:

'The forms and reports which Mr ... is required to submit are creating unacceptable stress and must be reduced if his health is not to suffer further.'

If you feel any sympathy at all with these two salesmen, get out of Selling; it's not your kind of business. Paper work – the right kind of paperwork – is essential. Get organized to chase business, not just will-o'-the-wisps.

But don't computerize it all. That's really playing into the competition's hands. Computers and salesforces just don't go together. All the reasons would take another book. Until it's written, you'll just have to take my word for it.

We need to plan our work …

… and then

Chapter 5
Working Smart

In 1974, a detailed survey was made of 1,100 industrial salesmen. It was found that each salesperson handles an average of 214 accounts. Of these 111 were active customers and 103 were prospective customers.

On each call, the salesperson talked to an average of four people.

He averaged 8.4 calls per working day.

He worked an average of 9 hours 15 minutes per day.

Of this 9 hours 15 minutes:

- 41 per cent was spent face-to-face with customers.
- 33 per cent was spent travelling.
- 20 per cent was spent on paperwork and administration.
- 5 per cent was spent servicing.

In 1991, the journal PC Management reported on a survey by JTM Business consultants, Manchester that (excluding retail, home improvements and life insurance) the average field salesperson was now spending his time as follows:

- 10 per cent face-to-face with customers
- 21 per cent other customer contact (telephone)
- 35 per cent travelling and waiting
- 16 per cent administration
- 17 per cent preparing quotations
- 1 per cent service work.

No surprises in these figures. Face-to-face selling time is reducing all the time as paper work and admin rise steadily. Travelling and waiting time remain about constant, but wouldn't it be wonderful if this enormous chunk of time could be reduced. That is a terrific slice out of the working day. Over 3 hours in the car, time that might have been more usefully spent talking to another customer.

Which is why Territory Planning is important.

Rules for Territory Planning

Just because the salesperson has been given that large slice of territory doesn't mean he has to cover *all* of it. Unless, of course, his competitors are doing just that.

He needs to get himself a large scale map of the territory, mount it on a sheet of pinboard or insulation board, cover it with a sheet of clear plastic, and acquire a quantity of map pins of various colours.

He needs to classify all his customers and prospective customers into groups, according to potential business, and allocate a pin colour to each group. For example:

Red … Major 'A' grade account
Blue … Average 'B' grade account
Green … Small 'C' grade account
Yellow … Occasional 'D' grade account
White … Prospect

Now let's go step by step through the procedure of what to do with the map and the coloured pins.

1. Pinpoint Home Base with a large knobbly pin, different from all the others.

2. Pinpoint with an appropriately coloured pin, the exact positions of all the customers and prospective customers on the map. These indicate all the places the salesperson has to travel to (see below.)

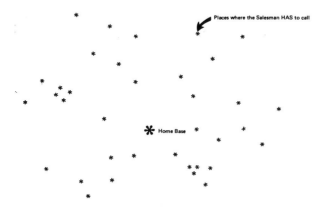

Places where the Salesman HAS to call

Home Base

3. Using a water-based felt pen, lightly draw in daily routes on the plastic sheet covering the map, starting and finishing at the Home Base, and covering all the pins sticking in the map (see below).

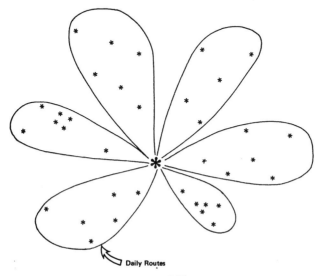

Daily Routes

I don't know any salesperson who got his routes right on the first try, so don't give up too early. Rub out the lines and start again.

The salesperson then has a map showing the part of his territory that he *has* to cover – those areas where his customers and known prospects are situated.

The secret from then on is quite simple – only look for new prospects *within* the daily routes. Leave companies outside these routes alone until there are no new ones left to call on within the routes.

Of course, quite often the salesperson will receive an enquiry from a company outside his route plan. Then he makes an appointment and travels over from the closest part of his nearest daily route, the next time he is in that sector of the territory.

If this new company turns out to be a waste of time, the salesperson writes it off his map. If, on the other hand, it turns out to be a sizeable potential customer, he may need to alter one of his daily routes to include the new call, or start a new route to cope most effectively.

If he had to start a new route, he then looks for five or six more prospects within the new route, as fast as he can to make the route a worthwhile full day's work.

In this way, the overall Territory Plan is continuously updated. The salesperson will find that this necessary updating will also extend the time-scale for him to get round every customer. But the order of magnitude we are talking about only changes a month to five weeks, or a year to 14 months or so. No customer will ever notice the difference.

Major Roads

Many salespeople use major roads as boundaries to sectors of their territories. Normally, however, roads are far more useful as spines, forming the centre of a sector, not the extremity. This is because companies tend to build factories near to major roads, not in the middle of farmland. So maybe the farmland, the river, or the forest, is a better boundary. Who cares it if cannot be clearly defined? Nobody is going near it anyway.

The daily routes we have so far used can be drawn on the map as leaf shaped, with a major road as the spine. The salesperson can then operate on a daily 'There-and Back' system, calling on companies on the left of the major road during the morning, stopping for lunch of a pie, pint and peppermint, at the outermost point of the route, and travelling back to base during the afternoon, calling on companies on the other side of the major road – but STILL his left.

The diagram below illustrates the method. It is highly praised by the road safety organizations because the salesperson does not even have to make a right-hand turn across the major road. Except before lunch, that is. Note that the watering places are all sited on the right of the road, when travelling from Home Base. Thus, the Salesperson always makes his right-hand turn when sober. (sic)

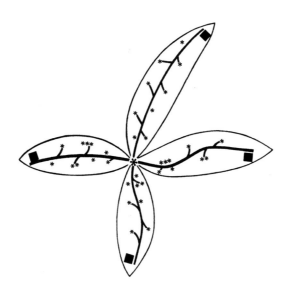

Having sorted out all his daily routes, the salesperson now has to work out his cycle of coverage, that is the order in which he uses the routes, so that he is never far away from any part of his territory for more than a few days at a time.

To illustrate the system, we will change the rules slightly, and use routes that are isolated islands instead of loops from Home Base and back. The way of working is just the same, only the salesperson needs to get up earlier and travel further to his first call of the day.

The diagram below illustrates a territory with 18 daily routes, which has been sectored to give a cycle of coverage of one week.

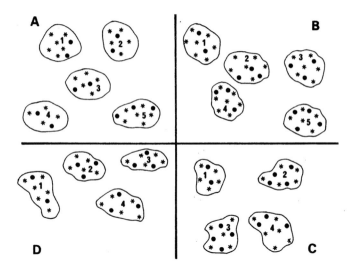

The salesperson calls in route A1 on Monday, B1 on Tuesday, C1 on Wednesday, D1 on Thursday and is back in sector A, calling in route A2, on the Friday. The next Monday he is in B2, Tuesday in C2 and so on.

There are deliberately four sectors and not five to avoid the salesperson finding himself in the same sector, on the same day of the week, every week. If this happened, a particular customer who was in sector A and was always out on a Monday, would never be seen. The same system can be used for many more than four sectors. The diagram below shows a plan for a two-week cycle, with 10 sectors and using a sequence of GBIECAHFDJ, or similar.

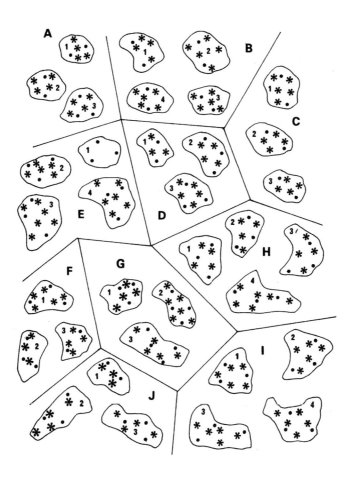

For larger territories, several planning systems can be combined. For example, the diagram below shows a territory where the major road dividing sectors G and H is 150 miles long. Sectors ABC and D operate on a weekly cycle, but for one week in every month, the salesperson spends a whole day in sector G, stays overnight in sector E, covers sector E and F on Tuesday and Wednesday (plus Thursday if necessary) and journies back through sector H on the next day. On this basis, customers in sectors E and F receive a call every two months, and customers in sectors G and H receive a call every month. Sectors ABC and D receive more concentrated coverage and the salesperson will normally be Home Based at B2 or 3, or C1 or 2.

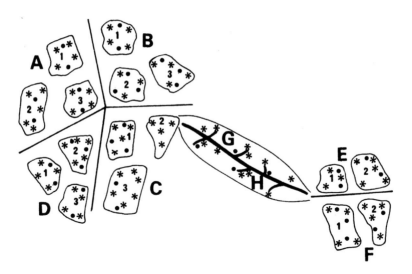

Organizing to Make Quota

Every salesperson needs a Target, or Quota, to aim for. Without a Quota, the whole job is a game of blind-man's bluff.

Any salesperson who hasn't got a quota should ask his Sales Manager for one. If the request is greeted with a blank stare and a grunt, 'Whad'ya mean, a Quota!', the salesperson should set his own, and then tell the Sales Manager what Quota he has set.

So let's assume there is a Quota, and that the salesperson is sitting down, just before the start of the selling year, to work out what he has to do to attain it.

First, the salesperson needs to delve into his records for some numbers:

1. How many customers does he have who are likely to buy again during the next year?

2. How much business does he expect from each customer?

3. How many calls can he make in a year?

4. What are his performance ratios and average order values for the current year?

Then he needs to work out the sums. Here is an example that I did for myself, quite a few years ago, when I was selling plastics.

Working the Figures

1. My turnover target for the coming year = £100,000.
2. It is divided into £80,000 from my existing customers, and £20,000 from new prospects.
3. From my past performance, I average 5 *calls per day* or *100 calls per month*.
4. My average order value over the past year for new accounts (that is, total income from new accounts divided by new accounts opened) is £2000.

5. Looking at past figures, I can put my existing customers into three priority categories: A, B and C (in descending order of importance).
6. Using these categories, I can allocate call frequencies:

Customer Category	Number of Existing Customers	Call Rate
A	10	Each month
B	30	Once every 2 months
C	120	Once every 3 months

7. Taking this a little further:

    'A' customers need 10 calls per month total
    'B' customers need 15 calls per month total
    'C' customers need 40 calls per month total
    = 65 calls per month for existing customers.

8. Compared with my average of 100 calls per month, this means I have 35 calls per month spare to get my prospect business.
9. Conclusion

    £80,000 business from existing customers needs 65 calls per month;

    £20,000 new business from prospects to be obtained from 35 calls per month...

    which seems reasonable as generally I have to put more effort into getting new business.

10. At a new business order value of £2000, I have to open 10 new accounts to make my new business target of £2000.
11. From past performance statistics I currently achieve two ratios:

    Five first calls on Prospects : One Proposal
    Four proposals: One order

12. This means that to open 10 new accounts, I have to find 10 x 4 x 5 = 200 prospects, or 200/10 or approximately 20 prospects per month (allowing for 10 months selling time in the average year.
13. I have to call three times on average on each new prospect.
14. This means 20 x 3 = 60 calls per month to get 10 new business orders, total value £20,000.
15. But 60 calls per month is quite incompatible with the 35 I have available.
16. What can I do about it?
    A Abandon planning? No, that's negative.
    B Reduce my miles per call, and hence increase my calls per day? Possible, I'll look at it.
    C Reduce targets? No, that's negative.
    D Less customers? No, that reduces my selling chances and could make matters worse. Leave this till later.
    E Improve my performance? Yes, be more effective, more efficient.

Personal performance

17. Suppose I really worked at the prospecting methods and the pre-call research. I ought to be able to improve first calls on prospects: proposals from 5:1 to 4:1.
18. Suppose I improved my proposal format and then used it on selected prospects as a closing tool, I could perhaps improve proposals: orders from 4:1 to 3:1.
19. In fact, my improved prospecting should itself increase the chances of the proposals being accepted.
20. With this improved performance, the number of prospects I need to get the same business is reduced to 10 x 3 x 4 = 120 prospects

= 12 prospects per month

= 36 calls per month.

21. This at least matches my spare allocation of 35 calls per month.

Fewer Customers

22. Maybe not as silly as it sounds. Suppose I re-categorized on the basis of potential business, rather than what we've had in the past? That means I must improve my forecasting techniques, but what would it mean?

23. Really my category C customers are what's left after selecting A and B. With more thought, I think I could reduce that figure of 120 to 75; after all, we haven't had much from them at best, and that's been thinly spread over the two years I've been in the territory.

24. That changes the arithmetic of items 6-9:

Customer Category	Number of Customers	Call Rate	Calls per month
A	10	Each month	10
B	30	Once every 2 months	15
C	75	Once every 3 months	25
	115		50

or 50 calls per month for customers (£80,000)

50 calls per month for prospects (£20,000)

25. Compared with my planned figure of 36 calls per month on prospects, I now have 14 calls per month spare for contingencies. That's equivalent to three days per month.

26. Of course, I won't just drop those 45 customers from category C; I'll put them in a new category, D, of 'those to be phoned or written to; even visited if circumstances permit'. I can use some of the spare three days per month for this.

Customers

27. Why should my existing customers get second-best treatment?
28. Suppose I treated them with the same thoroughness as prospects, instead of taking them too much for granted.
29. I wonder if they've thought that's how I treat them?
30. Right! Now how much business from *my* customers have I lost to competitors? How much more could I retrieve if I made an extra effort in keeping up with my customers' own development, and made better proposals for my solutions to their problems?

Remember

Better planning and improved performance give better results *in less time* (see items 17-20). No salesperson can afford *not* to plan and improve!

A salesperson needs to grow in terms of planning and improvement as his experience lengthens. The two do not necessarily go hand in hand! He needs to measure *his* performance to see if he is getting better at his job.

The figures in this example worked for me. Any salesperson reading this should use his *own* figures, of course, when *organizing to make his own Quota.*

Call Plans

Every salesperson should plan ahead at least one week, and have clearly in his mind where he will be calling during the following week – and why. This plan should be sent to head office or regional office so that it is in the right hands by the commencement of business for the week in question.

The 'right hands' belong to the person or persons who receive telephone calls from customers, and who often have to commit a salesperson to making an emergency call at very short notice. Give these persons a detailed plan of where the salesperson will be during the next five days, and there is far less chance of an emergency call that sends him 200 miles in the opposite direction.

Putting together a Call Plan is very simple. Remember – calls on prospects should be given priority when making appointments. Old established customers are much easier to call on without notice or with a postcard reminder.

Finally, if necessary, allow a half-day, say on Tuesday or Thursday afternoon, for emergency calls. Make no appointments on these half days, but plan some cold calls just in case the emergency calls do not arise. Then make sure the persons at head office try their best to book the emergency calls into these particular afternoons.

The example opposite shows a well-thought-out Call Plan.

Total Rate and Mix

Companies have the same problem that husbands have – especially if the husbands are salespeople.

Imagine the salesperson who is down on his orders, being called into the Sales Manager's office for a rocket.

'Don't worry,' the salesperson explains. 'I know things are quiet at the moment, but next month, we'll get Snooks, Bloggs and Imperial Cloggs, and it's all going to be lovely.'

'I believe you,' says the Sales Manager. 'Tell you what we'll do. We'll pay you a third of your salary this month, and make up the balance when those orders are in.'

Any salesperson would go through the roof at this sort of treatment.

'You can't do that,' he would rave. 'I've got a mortgage to pay, food and clothes to buy, a wife and kids to keep ...'

So how different is the company? It has a mortgage to pay (the works), and probably a bank overdraft. It has food and clothes to buy (raw materials and components and plant and equipment and toilet rolls and ...). It has a family to support (all its employees). So what

CALL PLAN 1–5 OCTOBER SALESMAN J. WATSON

TIME	APPT OR COLD	COMPANY	CONTACT	TELEPHONE NUMBER	AIM OF CALL
MONDAY					
9.30	A	PRESSED STEEL	J. BLACK	021 338 1862	DISCUSS QUOTE
11.30	C	POTTERSBY & Co	M/D		FACTORY EXT. PLANNED
2.00	C	J&B. ENG.	E. JONES		REF STOCK ORDER
3.45	A	HEREFORDS	R. WATSON	021 338 6464	RENEWAL OF VALVE CONTRACT
TUESDAY					
9.00	C	BAYTON RD. EXHALL	C/C		INDUSTRIAL ESTATE.
11.00	A	FISHER & WADE	E. SAMSON	0203 83789	ENQ. FOR PUMPS RE. AD IN JRN.
2.00	C	CONTINUE C/C EXHALL			
4.00	A	EXHALL TOOLS	R. FRANKS	0203 57651	DISCUSS NEW VALVE
WEDNESDAY					
9.00	A	COLLECT S/N AT BR STATION			
9.30	A	JONES & PRATT LTD	N. SMYTHE	0203 35221	NEW CONTRACT FOR OEM PUMP UNITS
2.00	A	DROP FORGINGS LTD	J. HINKLEY	0203 43355	FOLLOW UP AMENDED QUOTE
3.00	A	F. LACEY & Co.	L. BRIGGS	0203 67652	DISCUSS NEW VALVE
4.00	C	ARUNDEL DEVEL'TS	MNG DIR.		BUILDING NEW WORKS
THURSDAY					
9.30	A	HQ. PRODUCT TRAINING ON ETZ VALVE ↓			
FRIDAY					
10.00	A	BSC TUBES	M. DALY	CORBY 57221	COMMISSIONING NEW PLANT.
11.30	A	ANNEX MACS LTD	A. ROSS	56652	FOLLOW UP QUOTE
2.00	A	NOVA LIGHT UNITS	D. DAVIES	59241	DISCUSS NEW VALVE
4.00	A	SILVER POWER OILS	N. JENKINS	59911	MORE SPARE STOCKS FOR MAIN UNITS

ADVANCE APPOINTMENTS

DATE	TIME	COMPANY	CONTACT	AIM OF CALL
OCT 18	9.00	S.T. VALVES B'HAM	J. STANBRIDGE	NEW VALVE
OCT 26	2.15	BREEDONS N'TON	C. WHITE	" "

does the company do when it cannot get its money regularly, month by month?

One of three things:

1. Draw on its cash reserves.
2. Borrow (if it has any assets left).
3. Go bust.

Long before a crisis like this, the company has stopped paying its suppliers. So the extended credit disease gets worse and the supplying companies find themselves in the same boat.

The responsibility for seeing that money comes in to the company steadily and regularly lies squarely on the salesperson's shoulders. It all starts with the order intake.

Of course, the salesperson cannot influence precisely when a customer will place an order. This is fraught with intangibles and factors beyond his control.

But he can avoid a hiccup occurring in the order intake, and thus the cash flow, simply by stopping the all-too-human practice of waking up on a sunny Monday morning and saying:

'I don't feel like prospecting this week. I'll follow up a few quotations instead, and do the prospecting next week'.

Let me tell you a true story about a company in Sheffield that had a problem. I was called in to help sort things out, to be greeted by a very worried managing director, who informed me that the company had a rather pronounced seasonal demand. The order intake graph looked like Pamela Anderson sunbathing.

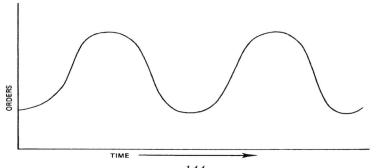

As the products were highly diversified, from chains, pallets, fabrications, and tanks to Goliath cranes, I was quite intrigued by the thought of a seasonal demand of such regularity and proportions. So I started digging.

It took all of three weeks to get to the root of the problem – and it will take five years at least to correct it and put the company back on an even keel.

Here's what happened.

At a time just a few months before the end of a particular financial year, the managing director, and accountant and also the major shareholder, generated himself a complex about take-overs. He'd lie in his bath with the adrenalin pounding through his body, reading the *Financial Times*, worrying about the state of his company and imagining that it was ripe for a swift bid from the competition.

The complex grew to overpowering proportions, so much so that the managing director started figuring how much he'd get for his shareholding when the take-over came about.

'Not enough,' he reckoned. So he set about re-shaping the asset and financial position of the company. 'What we need is a fatter order book,' he decided. 'That'll put the asking price up a bit.'

So he called the sales manager into his office. 'George,' he said, 'We need more orders before the end of the year. Get your salespeople to drop what they're doing and concentrate on securing firm orders. I want to see that order book full by December 31'.

This sounded reasonable to George, so he phoned all his salespeople and passed on the necessary instructions. And the order graph shot up (see overleaf).

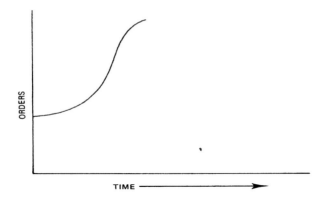

A short while later, the managing director, complex totally vanished, called the sales manager into his office, poured him a whisky and said, 'George, you're doing a fine job. Keep this up and there's a seat on the Board for you'.

Shortly afterwards, the order intake graph plummeted downwards (see below).

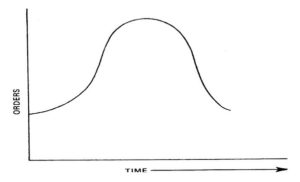

Hysterical, the managing director again faced George. 'I don't know what you're trying to do to this company, but if it isn't rectified fast now's a good time to start taking *The Daily Telegraph.*'

A swift stimulating kick to the salespeople and shortly afterward, up went the graph again – but this time by coincidence, not with malice aforethought.

By this time, of course, the damage was done. Nothing, but nothing could stop the rise and fall of the order intake graph. And all because of the managing director's complex.

What had happened was frighteningly simple. It could happen in any company and for many different reasons.

Given the initial instructions to drop everything else and concentrate on getting orders, every single person on the salesforce was doing the same thing at the same time – chasing up all the outstanding quotations (the only way to get orders quickly in Industrial Selling).

And they succeeded in closing quite a few. Not all of them, but enough to send the graph rocketing upwards.

Which was fine – until they ran out of outstanding quotations. Then they had to spend a period of time generating fresh enquiries to get to quotation stage. And during this period, very few orders could be secured, so down came the graph again.

You see, every product has a cycle time – the time it takes on average to generate an enquiry and process it to the point where the order is placed.

This cycle time is exceptionally hard to change. So if an entire salesforce does the same thing at the same time, the result is a similar-sized reaction at some future point in the time cycle. It's a bit like Newton said – for every action there is an equal and opposite reaction. Like thumping a half-full bag of grain. If you push a dent in one part, a bulge will form in another.

Let's get back to the salesperson who, one sunny Monday morning, said he'd follow up all his quotations and leave the prospecting until later. He was generating his own personal 'seasonal demand' graph. If every salesperson in his salesforce had said the same thing at the same time, the result would have been the same as for the poor old Sheffield company.

It's that simple to perpetrate.

The solution? Every week a salesperson should make an even number of all the types of calls he has to make. He has prospecting, surveys, demonstrations, following up quotations, and a few others. They should be spread evenly through each week. They should not be grouped together and mopped up one group at a time.

Just by doing this, he'll forestall all risk of generating his own personal 'seasonal demand'.

Order intake, of course, comes well before Cash Flow in terms of the time cycle. Any particular order that is received has to be manufactured, delivered and then invoiced. Some indefinite time after that, the customer pays. So in money terms, any 'seasonal demand' in order intake will have a delayed-action effect on the Cash Flow.

Any sales manager who buries his head in the sand like an ostrich and says he'll worry about Cash Flow when next year comes around, may be in for a surprise next week – when last year's incentive scheme really has its effect.

'Getting from Not Good Enough to Excellent is easy if we break the task down into 48 small pieces and get our teeth into them one at a time.'

John Fenton

Chapter 6

Monitoring your Personal Performance

Okay, so you're a Positive (and if you weren't before you started reading this book, I'll bet you are now). That's great. You're already ahead of the game, because you're one the salespeople that the buyers like best.

But Selling is a tough, competitive business. To make sure your company and, by implication, you keep moving ahead, you have to keep working at it. Rather like a shark, if you're not constantly moving forward, you're dead in the water.

How are you going to keep moving forward? How are you going to assess your performance, both overall and in terms of each of the many, many individual elements that make up your job? How can you make sure that you maintain your performance? How can you make improvements in a coherent and continuous way?

The answer is to monitor your performance in a highly detailed and quantitative way, and on a regular basis. What you have to do is break down your job into its component parts, work to improve weak areas, and organize yourself to become better all round. Make small improvements in every aspect of your selling activity and your results will improve more than you would have thought possible.

This may sound a tall order when you're, no doubt, working flat out just to maintain your performance, but it's easy when you use the PERSONAL PERFORMANCE MONITOR. This categorizes the various aspects of the work involved in Selling into **Activities**, **Skills**, **Knowledge** – and gives you a way to assess your performance in each area realistically.

PERSONAL PERFORMANCE MONITOR — ACTIVITY

NOT GOOD ENOUGH	GOOD ENOUGH	EXCELLENT	SCORES
I seldom plan for maximum calls and minimum miles `1 2 3 4 5 6 7 8 9 10 11 12`	I often plan for maximum calls and minimum miles `1 2 3 4 5 6 7 8 9 10 11 12`	I always plan for maximum calls and minimum miles `1 2 3 4 5 6 7 8 9 10 11 12`	Month 1 __ = 16
I seldom prepare a call plan `1 2 3 4 5 6 7 8 9 10 11 12`	I often prepare a detailed call plan one week ahead `1 2 3 4 5 6 7 8 9 10 11 12`	I always prepare a detailed call plan one week ahead `1 2 3 4 5 6 7 8 9 10 11 12`	Month 2 __ = 16
I seldom make appointments or send postcards `1 2 3 4 5 6 7 8 9 10 11 12`	I often make appointments and send postcards `1 2 3 4 5 6 7 8 9 10 11 12`	I maximise appointments and postcards `1 2 3 4 5 6 7 8 9 10 11 12`	Month 3 __ = 16
I often fail to follow up leads `1 2 3 4 5 6 7 8 9 10 11 12`	I occasionally fail to follow up leads within 2 days `1 2 3 4 5 6 7 8 9 10 11 12`	I always follow up leads within 2 working days `1 2 3 4 5 6 7 8 9 10 11 12`	Month 4 __ = 16
I seldom check anything beforehand `1 2 3 4 5 6 7 8 9 10 11 12`	I often check most things before a customer demonstration `1 2 3 4 5 6 7 8 9 10 11 12`	I always check everything before giving a customer demonstration `1 2 3 4 5 6 7 8 9 10 11 12`	Month 5 __ = 16
I occasionally attain territory targets `1 2 3 4 5 6 7 8 9 10 11 12`	I often attain territory targets by total sales `1 2 3 4 5 6 7 8 9 10 11 12`	I always strive to attain my territory targets by total, rate and mix `1 2 3 4 5 6 7 8 9 10 11 12`	Month 6 __ = 16
I seldom personally present quotations `1 2 3 4 5 6 7 8 9 10 11 12`	I often personally present quotations `1 2 3 4 5 6 7 8 9 10 11 12`	I strive to personally present every written quotation `1 2 3 4 5 6 7 8 9 10 11 12`	
I seldom complete the call report during calls `1 2 3 4 5 6 7 8 9 10 11 12`	I often complete the call report while with the customer `1 2 3 4 5 6 7 8 9 10 11 12`	I always strive to complete the call report while with the customer `1 2 3 4 5 6 7 8 9 10 11 12`	

Month 7	Month 8	Month 9	Month 10	Month 11	Month 12
── = 16	── = 16	── = 16	── = 16	── = 16	── = 16

Negative (1...)	Middle	Positive (...12)
I am reluctant to chase late payments	I am generally good at chasing late payments	I continually liaise with other departments to ensure best customer relations and cash flow
1 2 3 4 5 6 7 8 9 10 11 12	1 2 3 4 5 6 7 8 9 10 11 12	1 2 3 4 5 6 7 8 9 10 11 12
I seldom ask for references before opening a new account	I often ask for references before opening a new account	I always check credit worthiness before opening a new account
1 2 3 4 5 6 7 8 9 10 11 12	1 2 3 4 5 6 7 8 9 10 11 12	1 2 3 4 5 6 7 8 9 10 11 12
On exhibition stand duty I seldom secure names before giving out literature	I occasionally fail to secure visitors' names before giving out literature	I always secure customer name, address and reason for interest before giving literature
1 2 3 4 5 6 7 8 9 10 11 12	1 2 3 4 5 6 7 8 9 10 11 12	1 2 3 4 5 6 7 8 9 10 11 12
I hardly ever secure customer testimonials	I secure two or three good customer testimonials a year	I always secure at least one good customer testimonial letter every month
1 2 3 4 5 6 7 8 9 10 11 12	1 2 3 4 5 6 7 8 9 10 11 12	1 2 3 4 5 6 7 8 9 10 11 12
I seldom read anything relevant to the business	I often read the trade press	I continually monitor local newspapers and trade press for info on customers and markets
1 2 3 4 5 6 7 8 9 10 11 12	1 2 3 4 5 6 7 8 9 10 11 12	1 2 3 4 5 6 7 8 9 10 11 12
I never ask for management back-up	I often ask for management back-up when all else has failed	I always ask for management support when necessary to clinch an order
1 2 3 4 5 6 7 8 9 10 11 12	1 2 3 4 5 6 7 8 9 10 11 12	1 2 3 4 5 6 7 8 9 10 11 12
I seldom participate, except critically and negatively	I often participate actively at company sales meetings	I always participate positively at company sales meetings
1 2 3 4 5 6 7 8 9 10 11 12	1 2 3 4 5 6 7 8 9 10 11 12	1 2 3 4 5 6 7 8 9 10 11 12
I am not always well turned out and a credit to the company	I am generally well turned out and a credit to the company	I am always well turned out, fit and fresh and a credit to the company
1 2 3 4 5 6 7 8 9 10 11 12	1 2 3 4 5 6 7 8 9 10 11 12	1 2 3 4 5 6 7 8 9 10 11 12

PERSONAL PERFORMANCE MONITOR

NOT GOOD ENOUGH	GOOD ENOUGH	EXCELLENT	SKILLS / SCORES
I am often late [1 2 3 4 5 6 7 8 9 10 11 12]	Most times I am punctual [1 2 3 4 5 6 7 8 9 10 11 12]	I always aim to be punctual and allow for the unexpected [1 2 3 4 5 6 7 8 9 10 11 12]	**Month 1**
I often fail to make a good first impression [1 2 3 4 5 6 7 8 9 10 11 12]	Most times I make a good first impression [1 2 3 4 5 6 7 8 9 10 11 12]	I always make the best possible first impression [1 2 3 4 5 6 7 8 9 10 11 12]	___ = 16
I seldom establish the customer's objectives [1 2 3 4 5 6 7 8 9 10 11 12]	I occasionally fail to establish the customer's objectives [1 2 3 4 5 6 7 8 9 10 11 12]	I always establish the customer's objectives as early as possible [1 2 3 4 5 6 7 8 9 10 11 12]	**Month 2**
I seldom establish the customer's criteria for ordering [1 2 3 4 5 6 7 8 9 10 11 12]	I often establish the customer's criteria for ordering [1 2 3 4 5 6 7 8 9 10 11 12]	I always establish the customer's criteria for ordering [1 2 3 4 5 6 7 8 9 10 11 12]	___ = 16
I would rather tell than ask questions [1 2 3 4 5 6 7 8 9 10 11 12]	I often ask open-ended questions [1 2 3 4 5 6 7 8 9 10 11 12]	I always ask open-ended, quality and positive questions when seeking information [1 2 3 4 5 6 7 8 9 10 11 12]	**Month 3**
I handle some objections adequately [1 2 3 4 5 6 7 8 9 10 11 12]	I handle most objections successfully [1 2 3 4 5 6 7 8 9 10 11 12]	I always handle objections skilfully, leaving the customer satisfied [1 2 3 4 5 6 7 8 9 10 11 12]	___ = 16 / **Month 4**
I go for the order whatever the cost [1 2 3 4 5 6 7 8 9 10 11 12]	I often defend prices and try to avoid excessive discounts [1 2 3 4 5 6 7 8 9 10 11 12]	I always sell prices positively and minimise discounts [1 2 3 4 5 6 7 8 9 10 11 12]	**Month 5** / ___ = 16
Most times I settle for what the customer offers [1 2 3 4 5 6 7 8 9 10 11 12]	I often seek to add value to orders [1 2 3 4 5 6 7 8 9 10 11 12]	I always look for opportunities to add value to every order [1 2 3 4 5 6 7 8 9 10 11 12]	**Month 6** / ___ = 16

154

Month 7	Month 8	Month 9	Month 10	Month 11	Month 12
$\dfrac{\quad}{16} =$	$\dfrac{\quad}{16} =$	$\dfrac{\quad}{16} =$	$\dfrac{\quad}{16} =$	$\dfrac{\quad}{16} =$	$\dfrac{\quad}{16} =$

Item 1

I seldom worry about costs	I am generally concerned to keep selling costs within budget	I consistently strive to minimise selling costs and expenses
1 2 3 4 5 6 7 8 9 10 11 12	1 2 3 4 5 6 7 8 9 10 11 12	1 2 3 4 5 6 7 8 9 10 11 12

Item 2

I handle some complaints adequately	I handle most complaints successfully	I resolve speedily all complaints to the customer's complete satisfaction
1 2 3 4 5 6 7 8 9 10 11 12	1 2 3 4 5 6 7 8 9 10 11 12	1 2 3 4 5 6 7 8 9 10 11 12

Item 3

I often fail to recognise and act upon buying signals	I occasionally fail to recognise and act upon buying signals	I always recognise and act upon buying signals
1 2 3 4 5 6 7 8 9 10 11 12	1 2 3 4 5 6 7 8 9 10 11 12	1 2 3 4 5 6 7 8 9 10 11 12

Item 4

I seldom use the most appropriate method of closing the sale	I occasionally fail to use the most appropriate method of closing the sale	I ask for the (an) order on every call, using the most appropriate method of closing the sale
1 2 3 4 5 6 7 8 9 10 11 12	1 2 3 4 5 6 7 8 9 10 11 12	1 2 3 4 5 6 7 8 9 10 11 12

Item 5

I seldom agree objectives for the next call	I often agree objectives for the next call before departing	I always strive to agree objectives for the next call and make an appointment before departing
1 2 3 4 5 6 7 8 9 10 11 12	1 2 3 4 5 6 7 8 9 10 11 12	1 2 3 4 5 6 7 8 9 10 11 12

Item 6

I seldom ask for referrals	I often ask for referrals	I always ask for referrals
1 2 3 4 5 6 7 8 9 10 11 12	1 2 3 4 5 6 7 8 9 10 11 12	1 2 3 4 5 6 7 8 9 10 11 12

Item 7

I seldom mention terms of payment	I often agree terms of payment before accepting an order	I always agree terms of payment before accepting an order
1 2 3 4 5 6 7 8 9 10 11 12	1 2 3 4 5 6 7 8 9 10 11 12	1 2 3 4 5 6 7 8 9 10 11 12

Item 8

I go for the business whatever the cost	I generally try to be honest with the customers	I always act honestly and with integrity
1 2 3 4 5 6 7 8 9 10 11 12	1 2 3 4 5 6 7 8 9 10 11 12	1 2 3 4 5 6 7 8 9 10 11 12

PERSONAL PERFORMANCE MONITOR — KNOWLEDGE

NOT GOOD ENOUGH	GOOD ENOUGH	EXCELLENT
I seldom research the customer `1 2 3 4 5 6 7 8 9 10 11 12`	I often research the customer before the first call `1 2 3 4 5 6 7 8 9 10 11 12`	I always research the customer's business and buying methods before making first appointment `1 2 3 4 5 6 7 8 9 10 11 12`
I do not bother to check what information is needed before calls `1 2 3 4 5 6 7 8 9 10 11 12`	I have most of the relevant information for most calls `1 2 3 4 5 6 7 8 9 10 11 12`	I always have all the relevant information for every call `1 2 3 4 5 6 7 8 9 10 11 12`
I have some knowledge of most products (services) and their applications `1 2 3 4 5 6 7 8 9 10 11 12`	I am well informed about all products (services) and their applications `1 2 3 4 5 6 7 8 9 10 11 12`	I am fully conversant with all products (services) and their applications `1 2 3 4 5 6 7 8 9 10 11 12`
I know and use some selling points for most products (services) `1 2 3 4 5 6 7 8 9 10 11 12`	I know and use most selling points for all products (services) `1 2 3 4 5 6 7 8 9 10 11 12`	I know and use all selling points for all products (services) `1 2 3 4 5 6 7 8 9 10 11 12`
I seldom use my diary during calls `1 2 3 4 5 6 7 8 9 10 11 12`	I often use my diary during calls `1 2 3 4 5 6 7 8 9 10 11 12`	I have my diary to hand on every call `1 2 3 4 5 6 7 8 9 10 11 12`
I know little about competitors `1 2 3 4 5 6 7 8 9 10 11 12`	I know most of the principal competitors `1 2 3 4 5 6 7 8 9 10 11 12`	I know all principal competitors working in the territory and their strengths and weaknesses `1 2 3 4 5 6 7 8 9 10 11 12`
I seldom report on competitor activity `1 2 3 4 5 6 7 8 9 10 11 12`	I often report on competitor price changes `1 2 3 4 5 6 7 8 9 10 11 12`	I always report quickly and in detail any changes in competitor prices and activity `1 2 3 4 5 6 7 8 9 10 11 12`
I seldom ask why an order is lost `1 2 3 4 5 6 7 8 9 10 11 12`	I often ask why an order is lost `1 2 3 4 5 6 7 8 9 10 11 12`	I always find out why an order is lost to a competitor `1 2 3 4 5 6 7 8 9 10 11 12`

SCORES

Month 1	Month 2	Month 3	Month 4	Month 5	Month 6
— / 16	— / 16	— / 16	— / 16	— / 16	— / 16

| | Month 7 | = 16 | Month 8 | = 16 | Month 9 | = 16 | Month 10 | = 16 | Month 11 | = 16 | Month 12 | = 16 |

My customer records are not often up to date | 1 2 3 4 5 6 7 8 9 10 11 12

My customer records are mostly up to date | 1 2 3 4 5 6 7 8 9 10 11 12

My customer records are always accurate, neat and up to date | 1 2 3 4 5 6 7 8 9 10 11 12

I seldom record data on products (services) sold | 1 2 3 4 5 6 7 8 9 10 11 12

I record most data on products (services) sold for most customers | 1 2 3 4 5 6 7 8 9 10 11 12

I record full data on products (services) sold for every customer | 1 2 3 4 5 6 7 8 9 10 11 12

I pay little attention to customers' DMU | 1 2 3 4 5 6 7 8 9 10 11 12

I know something of most customers' DMU | 1 2 3 4 5 6 7 8 9 10 11 12

I know the structure and personnel of every customer decision making unit (DMU) | 1 2 3 4 5 6 7 8 9 10 11 12

I know little about customers' preferred call times | 1 2 3 4 5 6 7 8 9 10 11 12

I know the best day and time for most regular customer contacts | 1 2 3 4 5 6 7 8 9 10 11 12

I know the best day and time to call on every customer decision maker and decision influencer | 1 2 3 4 5 6 7 8 9 10 11 12

I know few possible outlets | 1 2 3 4 5 6 7 8 9 10 11 12

I know many of the possible outlets for the company's products | 1 2 3 4 5 6 7 8 9 10 11 12

I know most of the possible outlets in my territory for the company's products | 1 2 3 4 5 6 7 8 9 10 11 12

I know little about any of the possible outlets | 1 2 3 4 5 6 7 8 9 10 11 12

I have a firm idea of the probable potential of some of the possible outlets | 1 2 3 4 5 6 7 8 9 10 11 12

I have a firm idea of the probable potential of every possible outlet | 1 2 3 4 5 6 7 8 9 10 11 12

I am unhappy with my job, its status and the way it is done | 1 2 3 4 5 6 7 8 9 10 11 12

I enjoy my job and go along with how the company wants it done | 1 2 3 4 5 6 7 8 9 10 11 12

I have a firm belief in the value of my job and the way it is done | 1 2 3 4 5 6 7 8 9 10 11 12

I rarely read anything relevant to the job or business | 1 2 3 4 5 6 7 8 9 10 11 12

I often read books on business | 1 2 3 4 5 6 7 8 9 10 11 12

I continually read books on selling and related subjects | 1 2 3 4 5 6 7 8 9 10 11 12

ASK Yourself How You're Doing

All you have to do is make a regular monthly date to go through the 48 points (16 in each category) listed for Activities, Skills and Knowldege. This shouldn't take long, but it will involve some soul-searching and a little bit of calculation to work out your aggregate score. Don't begrudge the time it takes you to go through the PPM, remember: *It takes time to save time*. And what could save more time than to perform at an absolute optimum level?

This is how you do it. In month 1, first study carefully the 16 statements on the PPM Activity card. Whichever is the statement closest to your current performance (and please be honest with yourself) put a mark in the appropriate month 1 square.

Do the same for all 16 of the Activity elements listed on the card. When you have finished, total up your score for month 1 on Activity. Here's how you score:

> For each assessment of NOT GOOD ENOUGH, score 1 point
>
> For each assessment of GOOD ENOUGH, score 2 points
>
> For each assessment of EXCELLENT, score 3 points

Total up your points and enter this number in the month 1 Scores box on the right of the Activity card. Divide this number by 16 (the number of subjects on the card) to calculate your Average Activity Score for month 1. Work it out to two places of decimals.

Turn now to the Skills category and go through the process again, just as carefully. This is *your* performance you are examining.

Then do it all again for the Knowledge category.

You now have three average scores for month 1, and you can use this as a basis for making sure that you are

IMPROVING YOUR PERFORMANCE MONTH BY MONTH.

By now you should be realising just how valuable this PPM system is going to be to you, by helping you to quantify and plan a whole year's worth of improvement. As well as pinpointing exactly where you stand today in terms of your performance in no less than 48 elements of your work, the statements tell you what you should be doing to achieve EXCELLENT in every area.

Think about what you should be doing, then do it once. Go on, force yourself. It's bound to be toughest the first time, particularly if its something you avoid doing because you don't like it – like chasing late payments. Then do it again and again.

The only difference between an act and a habit is repetition.

Pretty soon you'll be developing habits that will boost your performance – and your commission.

Your first priority will be to work on any areas that you have identified as being NOT GOOD ENOUGH. Bring these up first to balance your performance. Obviously, your long-term goal has to be to improve all round so that you've scored a three, or EXCELLENT, in every category. But you don't need to do everything at once. Instead, select a few crucial elements each week and work at moving your performance towards EXCELLENT on these. The rest of the elements can wait for future weeks.

Review your progress each month. Decide how you are doing in the areas you've resolved to work on. Are you maintaining your standards all round? Are you turning good practice into a habit? Fill in your scores for Month Two in all categories and work out your average scores for each as before. If you move from one column to another, for example, from 'NOT GOOD ENOUGH' to 'GOOD ENOUGH', fill in the month square with a coloured pen or highlighter, so that your improvement stands out. When you calculate your totals for the end of the month, you should notice a modest improvement. If you can sustain your improvement and maintain performance in all other areas, you will be moving gradually towards achieving your goal – EXCELLENT – in every category.

ALL BUSINESS IS SHOW BUSINESS – AND YOUR ATTITUDE IS ALWAYS SHOWING

What could be more inspiring and impressive to the buyer than the attitude of someone who is always striving to make improvements in the way they do business and in the service they provide?

YOUR ATTITUDE DETERMINES YOUR ALTITUDE

And soon you'll be flying higher than you ever thought possible.

Yes we can!

Chapter 7

How to Stay Ahead and Grow While All Around You the Competitors are Falling Like Flies

Research carried out by John Fenton Training International plc and others, mainly using the membership of the Institute of Purchasing Management as the survey sample, came up with the following list:

The top 10 things business buyers dislike about salespeople:

1. They don't know anything about our business
2. They waste my time
3. They call too often
4. They don't call often enough
5. They miss appointments
6. They break promises
7. They overclaim
8. They don't have the authority to negotiate
9. They don't come to me first
10. They don't ask for the order.

What Customers *do* look for in the salespeople who visit them is: COMPETENCE.

It's pretty sobering, isn't it. But you can make sure that *you* are the competent salesperson, the one the buyers like, and consequently the one they want to buy from. It's up to you.

'When all is said and done, there's more said than done!'

When all is said and done; when you've read this last chapter, if all you do is say to yourself, 'I enjoyed that' and you put this book on your library shelf to gather dust forever, neither of us will have achieved much, will we?

Everything you need to know about Selling, to be able to make sure you stay ahead and grow, is in the four books in this Profession of Selling series. Everything you need to know to be able to change your attitude towards the job, work and success, is in this book.

Everything you need to know to be able to change from a Negative to a Positive, from a Sheep to a Wolf, from a Representative to a Professional Sales Executive, from being Poor to being Rich.

And if I may quote Mae West on this last point – and agree wholeheartedly with her – 'I've been rich and I've been poor and believe me baby, rich is best!'

If you're saying to yourself 'Yes, I see the point, but it looks too much like hard work and I'm busting a gut now, I've no time even to consider changing my way of working like this guy Fenton says I should' then let me present you with a kind of recap on the whole thing – something that originated from the Caterpiller Tractor Corporation as a rather unusual type of recruitment advertisement.

Wanted – a LAZY Salesperson

So lazy, he takes advantage of every sales aid provided by his company.

So lazy, he copies the methods of the most successful salespeople.

So lazy, he carefully plans his routes to hold travelling to a minimum.

So lazy, he concentrates his efforts on the customers and potential customers who represent the most business.

So lazy, he frequently makes appointments by phone so he won't be put through the trouble of calling on a customer who's unavailable.

So lazy, he keeps written records on each account so he won't have to strain his memory.

So lazy, he follows up immediately every lead from his company's sales promotion, figuring that these represent people who are ready to buy.

So lazy, he relies on testimonials, figuring that satisfied customers can say things for him that he can't say himself.

So lazy, he insists on getting a good night's sleep every night, especially exhibition week.

So lazy, he refuses to run errands for his wife during working hours.

If you come across such a person turn him in immediately. *Everybody* seems to be looking for him!

Absolutely right. Everybody *is* looking for him. There aren't many positively lazy salespeople about. So if you fear hard work, get your teeth into the techniques described in this book and do it the 'Lazy Salesperson' way.

Why are the Competitors Falling like Flies?

I weigh in at 12 stone 5. That's 168 pounds USA style. I fluctuate between 166lbs and 170lbs. As I write these last few pages I'm sitting on a hotel patio in Tenerife, and I'm looking down on a poolside filled with grotesquely overweight male and female bodies. I've been here only a week, yet I'm already struggling to keep within my limits. The food is fantastic, and I'm only human.

I used to be 14 stone. The motivation I needed to lose nearly two stone I got by looking ahead three months to the Sales Road Shows I was scheduled to run throughout the autumn – 12 shows across three months. Five hours on stage, just about non-stop. 'What if I keeled over after four hours?' I asked myself.

When you aim to put on a one man show and play to 2,000 people, I tell you, you generate the motivation to make sure it happens. I bought an exercise bike, a rowing machine, installed a 'Spa' hot bath and went on Judy Mazel's pineapple diet. Two miles on the bike every morning, half a pineapple and two cups of black tea (no milk or sugar) – nothing else until lunchtime, and in three months I was thinner and fitter than I'd ever been before, even as a teenager. Stamina energy was what I was building. The ability to keep going for long periods at full stretch. The less weight I carried, the easier it became.

I also already had a major asset in the way I coped with mental pressure. Everyone needs a way of winding down, a way of relieving the frustration of the bad working day, of being able to relax and banish away the problems of the week, so that they can begin again fresh the next morning. For some people it's classical music and a pair of high fidelity headphones. For others it's building model railways. For the more dynamic it's a game of squash in the evenings. I see that a touch too dangerous at 60. My pastime is a pretty comprehensive set of Ludwig drums and Paiste cymbals, wrapped round with 300 watts of pretty deafening stereo. My only danger is the amount of wax I generate in my ears, but beating hell out of a set of drums to the added therapy of music is right for me.

However you do it, you've got to be mentally and physically fit to succeed in this exciting business we call Selling.

You need a hobby, a way of relaxing from the pressure of business. One that fits your metabolism. But it cannot be a very time consuming one. You need all the time you can get for building your career.

Life is Full of Forks in the Road

And this is one of them!

Take the correct road at this fork and you'll never look back. Take the wrong road and you'll stay more or less where you are now, until you get to another fork in the road, further ahead.

Then you'll have another chance to choose the right road. And another chance at another fork in the road, even further ahead. That's life.

But all the time you're getting older. If you're also getting wiser, you'll know you should have taken maybe a different road at a fork in the road some way back. What this means is that now has to be a better time than the next fork, or next year, or next first of the month, doesn't it?

If you want it to happen; if you want to be successful, not average; if you want to be rich, not poor; if you want to beat the hell out of your competitors; you, no one else, you have got to make it happen.

It's *your* future!

You've got to overcome every bit of your natural resistance to change. Maybe you should remember that the only thing in life, other than death, that is permanent – is change.

Don't fight it. Practice instead the words of C. F. Kettering 'My interest is in the future, because I am going to spend the rest of my life there.

As you read this page, today is the beginning of the rest of your life. Live it successfully. Get great fun out of it. Do great business. Build great businesses. And leave your competitors far, far behind.

You can do it

Index